EIR (ISSN 0273-6314) *is published weekly
(50 issues), by EIR News Service, Inc.,
P.O. Box 17390, Washington, D.C. 20041-0390.
(703) 777-9451 ext. 415*

European Headquarters: E.I.R. GmbH, Postfach
Bahnstrasse 9a, D-65205, Wiesbaden, Germany
Tel: 49-611-73650
Homepage: http://www.eirna.com
e-mail: eirna@eirna.com
Director: Georg Neudecker

Montreal, Canada: 514-461-1557

Denmark: EIR - Danmark, Sankt Knuds Vej 11,
basement left, DK-1903 Frederiksberg, Denmark.
Tel.: +45 35 43 60 40, Fax: +45 35 43 87 57. e-mail:
eirdk@hotmail.com.

Mexico City: EIR, Sor Juana Inés de la Cruz 242-2
Col. Agricultura C.P. 11360
Delegación M. Hidalgo, México D.F.
Tel. (5525) 5318-2301
eirmexico@gmail.com

No More Assassinations Shut Down Obama

Shut Obama Down
To End his Murder Spree

Dec. 20—Russia's Ambassador to Turkey, Andrey G. Karlov, was shot dead yesterday, while delivering an address at the Contemporary Arts Center in Ankara. Turkish Interior Minister Suleyman Soylu later identified the attacker as a 22-year-old former police officer by the name of Mevlut Mert Altintas. According to news reports, he was heard shouting, "Don't forget Aleppo! Don't forget Syria! As long as our brothers are not safe, you will not enjoy safety."

In response to the attack, Turkish President Recip Erdogan, speaking on behalf of both himself and Russian President Vladimir Putin, denounced the assassination as an open "act of provocation" against Turkey-Russian relations. The assassination comes on the eve of a series of conferences aimed at resolving the Syrian crisis, between Turkey, Russia, Iran, and others, including both the Syrian government and moderate opposition.

Heightening global tensions, on the very same day as the Ankara shooting, a 25-ton truck ploughed into a crowded Christmas market in central Berlin, killing 12 people and injuring at least 48 others. On Tuesday, Dec. 20, a posting was made to the Amaq website of ISIL (the Islamic State of Iraq and the Levant), claiming responsibility for the Berlin attack. The posting stated, "A soldier of the Islamic State carried out the Berlin operation in response to appeals to target citizens of coalition countries."

Upon receiving the first reports of the Ankara assassination, statesman Lyndon LaRouche immediately stated, "Put Obama on the list of suspects." He also stated that the assassination itself was "a deliberate kind of kill—a set-up," and that the murder was "not just vengeance, it's a special operations act." He urged that authorities "run down the people involved in any way in this."

Obama Will Kill, Unless He Is Stopped

Three days prior to the Ankara shooting, Lyndon LaRouche had warned—after hearing a nationally broadcast interview given by President Obama on National Public Radio—that bloody, murderous actions by Obama could be expected in the days ahead. In that interview, Obama had specifically threatened action against Russia, asserting that Russia hacked Democratic National Committee computers. Obama raved, "I think there is no doubt that, when any foreign government tries to impact the integrity of our elections, that we need to take action, and we will, at a time and place of our choosing. Some of it may be explicit and publicized; some of it may not be, but Mr. Putin is well aware of my feelings about this, because I spoke to him directly about it."

In response to Obama's statements, Lyndon LaRouche said, "These words are a threat to murder people of importance. This is what Obama's stepfather taught him." LaRouche called on citizens to "watch this guy, so that he doesn't kill. He is publicly threatening the world. The nations of the planet are now threatened by Obama's plan for mass killing of people." Obama "is intrinsically a killer," as LaRouche put it.

Earlier, at his Dec. 16 White House Press Conference, Obama repeated his threat against "Russian hacking." He said that he told Russia "to stop it, and indicated there will be consequences when they do it.... Our goal continues to be to send a clear message to Russia." Further, Obama concurred with the CNN

White House reporter's summation, that "The President thinks Vladimir Putin authorized the hack."

All the evidence, however, shows that Obama's murderous provocations against Russia have nothing to do with alleged "hacking." Despite repeated requests from the House Intelligence Committee for the Obama Administration to provide evidence of the "hacking," all of the top Obama Administration intelligence officials have outright refused to go to Congress, declining even to appear in a close-door session. There have also been multiple indications that other intelligence agencies, including their top officials, do not agree with CIA Director John Brennan's conclusion about Russian hacking. So far, not one shred of evidence has been presented.

The actual danger, in this post-election environment, arises from Obama's predilection for murder—and the fact that he is soon to be out of office, where he will have neither executive powers nor protection from possible prosecution for his crimes.

Look at the Obama record. There are his Tuesday target meetings to draw up victim-lists for killing-by-drones. There are the continued deployments of American men and women to go to their harm and death, in U.S. military service, in the 16 years of Obama/Bush/British regime-change wars (Iraq, Afghanistan, Syria, Libya). Within the United States, death rates and drug overdoses are soaring as a result of the Obama economic disaster, which he calls a successful "recovery."

Look at Obama's history. Lyndon LaRouche has stressed many times that Obama comes by killing from his own upbringing. His stepfather, Lolo Soetoro in Indonesia, was a killer-operative in the subversion and slaughter (1965-66) to bring down the government of President Sukarno. Obama wrote in his autobiography of how he learned during that time, that killing the weak is what the strong do.

LaRouche noted that, "internationally right now, we have people leading a world program for development and peace [the Eurasian New Silk Road, with President Xi Jinping, along with President Putin and others], but Obama will not just let things get by peacefully. He will kill; then the problem comes in, and it's a bloody mess." LaRouche emphasized that, "The signals are all there. Obama has made it clear... Obama has made repeated efforts to show his readiness for large-scale killing in the United States and other nations." What needs to be done, is "to shut down Obama," to prevent what he intends to do.

EIR Contents

www.larouchepub.com Volume 43, Number 52, December 23, 2016

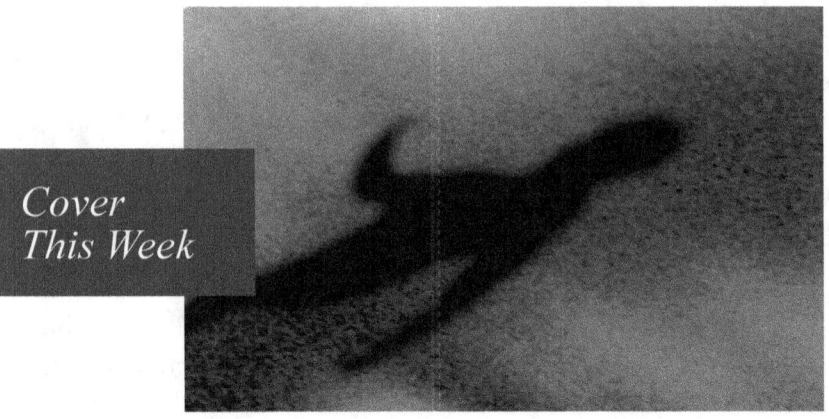

*Cover
This Week*

EIR will not skip its end-of-year issue, and will appear
on Dec. 30, 2016.

Helga Zepp-LaRouche: We Must Have Global Development, Not Geopolitics

The following is an edited transcript of the Question and Answer discussion period, following Helga Zepp LaRouche's speech, "Donald Trump and the New International Paradigm," delivered at a conference of the Schiller Institute in Copenhagen, Denmark on December 12, 2016.[1] To facilitate free discussion, the questioners are not identified, and the questions are summarized. The answers are complete.

Solidarité & Progrès
Helga Zepp-LaRouche

Question: About whether we can be optimistic about Trump's Presidency, because Trump is skeptical about climate change, is for trade war with China and Mexico, opposes the free trade deals, and has called for tearing up the nuclear deal with Iran.

Helga Zepp-LaRouche: I said earlier that the potentialities for change are there, but it depends, to a very large extent, upon us—what we do. When Trump got elected, my first response was, this is what I call the "dog pull-tail, let-go feeling." What I mean by that is that when you pull the tail of a dog—which you should never do, naturally—and you let go, the pain stops. When you pull, there is pain, and when you stop pulling, the pain goes away.

So, in a certain sense, the election of Trump was the tail let-go feeling, because we were on an immediate course toward World War III, and that was really the

primary point, because if Hillary Clinton would have been elected—unfortunately, Hillary Clinton, when she was in the Obama administration, transformed from being a relatively OK person; she was never great, but in 2008, she was relatively decent, compared to what she became, because she capitulated to Obama; and when she made this terrible statement, for example, in Libya, about the murder of Qaddafi, "We came, we saw, and he died." This is barbarism. Her behavior in the Benghazi case.

There were so many things where she became worse than Obama, almost. So the immediate thing was the big danger, that she would have continued the policies of Bush and Obama, in the confrontation with Russia and China; that this was stopped is, already, for the survival of civilization, the most important step.

Now, on these other points. Naturally, there is climate change. There is no question about it. But the question is, what is the cause of it? And the Schiller Institute had several conferences where we invited extremely important scientists who presented, beyond a doubt, that if you look at the last 500 million years in the history of the Earth, you have a continuous cycle of ice ages, of warming periods, of small ice ages, and the man-made component of climate change is absolutely negligible. It's a big fraud, for example, it's a big business. To sell CO_2 emission quotas, is like selling indulgences in the Middle Ages.

Obviously, there are climate changes, and some countries which have low coasts are very much affected; but then you have to adapt to these climate changes with modern technology, and you cannot solve the problem by going to electric cars, or going to decarbonization of the world economy. This is a big fraud, and I am not saying that Trump is saying this for all the right reasons; but the idea to impose measures implied by the "great transformation" Schellnhuber is talking

---

1. The full speech is printed in the December 16 issue of *EIR*, Volume 43, Number 51.

about—I mean these people do not want development.

We have been on this case for the last— as a matter of fact, we, the LaRouche movement, had a conception about the development of the world really starting at the end of the '60s.

I joined Mr. LaRouche because I went to China, Africa, other Asian countries, and I saw the horrible, horrible underdevelopment. So I came back from this trip, and I said, "I have to become political, because I want to change this." I could give you a long, long story of the many observations, because I went with a cargo ship, and when you go to these countries with a cargo ship, you get a quite different idea than if you go on a five-star cruise, and hotels. You see how the poverty affects people in their real lives. And I came back, and I looked at all the political movements, and I saw that LaRouche was the only one who said, "We have to have Third World development. We have to have technology transfer. We have to alleviate this poverty."

And we had a positive conception already in the '70s, and therefore, when the Club of Rome appeared, we immediately said, "This is a fraud." Because the Club of Rome said, "There are limits to growth. We have reached equilibrium. Until the year 1972, you could develop, but now, we have reached equilibrium, and we have to have sustainable development. We have to have appropriate technology." These notions did not exist before, because before, you had the idea of a UN Development Decade, where each decade, you would overcome the underdevelopment by qualitative jumps. And when we recognized this propaganda by the Club of Rome, we immediately said, "This is a complete fraud," and the people who wrote the book *Limits to Growth*, Meadows and Forrester…

Question: A followup about the Paris climate summit.

Zepp-LaRouche: I would like to give you written documentation afterwards of the studies that were made by these geologists, which are, without question, the explanation that climate change is not man-made. The anthropogenic aspect of it is so minuscule. Climate change has to do with the position of the Solar system in the Galaxy, which goes in cycles around a certain axis, and you can see that over 500 million years, the data confirm that you have these wide changes. Greenland is called Greenland, because it was green. There used to be vineyards. You had ice ages which completely covered the Earth, and the reason why I went into this longer history, is to show how the environmentalist movement was created with the attempt to keep development down, and climate change is just another expression of the same effort.

If you look at which firms are investing in solar parks, in wind parks, who is controlling the CO_2 emission trade, you have all the top hedge-funds in London and Wall Street. I can give you a lot of documentation about it, which does not mean that climate change is not real, because you have the rise of the oceans, and you have climate change, you have extreme weather, but that has been happening for hundreds of millions of years.

And, on the other points you raised—obviously, from our standpoint, the cancellation of NAFTA is a good thing, because NAFTA did not allow development for Mexico. As a matter of fact, NAFTA is the incarnation of the cheap labor production model of free trade. What you need is— especially countries which are not developed, you need protective tariffs for their own good. They have to develop a domestic market first. The booklet which I emphasized, which you should please read, *Against the Stream* [by von Kardorff], is one of many, but it is very condensed, and a very good book.

The question is: What is the source of wealth? Is the source of wealth cheap labor, to buy cheap raw materials, produce cheaply, and sell expensive? Is that the cause of wealth? No.

The only cause of wealth is the increase in the creativity of labor power. And a good government is, therefore, investing the maximum amount into education, into sponsoring the creativity of youth, of labor; and the more people in the labor force, by percentage, as engineers, scientists, the more productive the economy becomes.

And the free-trade system, of which NAFTA is just one example, did exactly the opposite. China, which was part of this in the beginning— the reason why China today has so many environmental problems, like smog, like a large amount of groundwater being contaminated, is the result of the fact that China, in the beginning of its industrialization, accepted being a cheap labor production place for the U.S. and for Europe. When I was in China, even in 1971, I visited some factories which were horrible. They were absolutely horrible. The working conditions were terrible, the labor force, which produced electrical devices for radios, it was horrible. They worked for 18 hours. No health system. It was just terrible. And that is how China developed in the first phase.

But then China, with Deng Xiaoping, started to recognize that that is the wrong way. So China is now on a completely different track. They are putting the maximum emphasis on science and technology, the increase of excellence. Last year, they produced 1 million scientists. That's double what the U.S. produced. Obviously, China is a larger country, but still. What will finally be decisive is the number of people who are creative. And that is why China, right now, has the best education system, because they have understood that the source of wealth is not raw materials. Is not trade conditions. It is the creativity of their own people. And that is a good thing. If we go to a system where we have a certain amount of protectionism, to protect the development of the domestic market, it is a good thing.

Creative Commons

Shanghai Tower under construction, April 12, 2011.

There is no danger of cutting [countries off from one another], because all of these infrastructure projects are connectivity. The world will be more connected than ever before. But this whole myth of free trade is really a very bad thing. It has been coined by the people who profit from it. That's why the world is in the condition it is right now, where the rich become richer, and the poor become poorer. The middle class is being destroyed all over the world. And I would really like to communicate with you so that we can deepen this dialogue.

On the Iran thing, I don't think he will break it, but that is my hope. I don't know.

So, I'm not saying he's a— as I said, Baron von Knigge would get a heart attack if he could hear Trump's speeches—but the world was in such a grip of evil, Satanic evil, that it is a good thing that there is a break, and the unfortunate thing, is that Europe is still in this grip.

You can see it. Von der Leyen, the German Defense Secretary, had the funniest reaction. The day after the election of Trump, she said "I am deeply shocked" about this election result, because nobody thought this would happen. Now, this same lady is now parading in Saudi Arabia with Deputy Crown Prince Salman bin Abdulaziz Al-Saud, and she isn't shocked. So, I don't know what's wrong with her. I think Saudi Arabia would be a good place to be shocked, or not even go there.

So, I have come to the conclusion that a lot of the

Europeans who react this way to the defeat of Hillary, are obeying another power in their head, and that power I call The British Empire, which is still in place, and it dominates Europe, and that is why they feel— I was asking myself, how come all of these politicians are so arrogant towards the new president of the U.S.? Because they were the boot-lickers of Washington until yesterday, and they would immediately do everything Washington would say and do, so I asked myself, 'Where is this sudden self-assertiveness coming from?' And the only explanation I came up with, was to say, they must have an idea that there is another power which is more powerful than Trump; otherwise, they wouldn't have this sudden arrogance.

And it is the British, because you will see tomorrow, there will be a federal press conference in Berlin, where a number of people will present their contribution to the German chairmanship of the G-20, which will take place in July in Hamburg. This will be Joachim Schellnhuber, the head of the German Advisory Council on Global Change (WBGU); this is the scientific advisory organization advising the German government. He put out this paper about "the great transformation," which we wrote about. You can look in the archive. He is the head of the idea of a de-carbonization of the world economy.

Now, if you de-carbonize the world economy, without having fusion—that would be one thing, to have fusion power in place; then you can talk about getting rid of fossil fuels—but without having fusion, and being against nuclear energy, fission, it means that you will reduce the world's population to one billion or less, because there is a direct correlation between the energy flux-density and the number of people you can maintain. Schellnhuber said that the carrying capacity of the Earth is maximum one billion people. He didn't say what he wants to do with the other six billion who are already here. If he would be consistent, he should hop away from this planet.

They will announce a sinister plan, to try to use the fact that many countries have environmental problems, to sneak in their anti-development programs. People should not be naïve, because not everybody thinks that population growth is a good thing. There are many people who think that each human being is a parasite, destroying nature. That is the image of man which many people have. The Greenies, for example.

First edition of Schiller's "William Tell."

We look at it in a different way. We think that the more people you have, the greater longevity you can have, division of labor; and a modern scientific society needs many people with a long life span. Because if you are in the Third World, and you die, and you have an average life expectancy of 40 years, or less, you cannot have scientists, because the production of a scientist takes 30-35 years, and if people then die right away, then you can't have a modern society.

So the more creative people you have, the better. Each human being is an incredible addition, because we are creative.

Tom Gillesberg: Schellnhuber, for his services, was appointed Commander of the Order of the British Empire (CBE), and for him, he personally has said, that the high-point of his existence was that the British Queen, personally, gave him the Order of the British Empire, for his efforts to reduce the possibility for mankind's survival, you could say. So it is connected with what you said.

Question: This is the best speech I have ever heard in my life. Is this a second American Revolution, and will the Federal Reserve, which is privately owned, be closed down? And will money be created for the benefit of all people, and not just the private Fed?

Zepp-LaRouche: I don't know, because, as I said, there are so many unknowns about Trump, and what he will do, and how it will play out. All I can say is, if Trump does not fulfill his promises, the same people who caused his election, will topple him. Because I don't think that this process, which is now underway, where ordinary people have just had it— if you think about the Declaration of Independence, it has this formulation that you will not bring down a government system for light reasons, but, if for a long time, the common good is being violated, then people have the right and duty to replace this government with a rightful one; and that idea I call natural law.

It's the same idea that Friedrich Schiller had in "Wilhelm Tell." This is a play he wrote, which takes place in Switzerland. There, the Hapsburg oligarch is also trampling on the rights of the Swiss people; then they unite with the Rütli Oath. Then there is a beautiful formulation which says, When the rights of the people are trampled upon, they have the right to appeal to Heaven, and grasp from thence their everlasting rights, which still inalienable hang on high, as inviolable as the stars themselves.

If you compare these two texts, the Declaration of Independence, and the Rütli Oath from Schiller's play, they are almost identical; and it's very clear that Schiller was inspired by the American Revolution when he wrote that play, because in his plays, there are many ideas which resonate with the American Revolution, and he actually wanted to emigrate at one point, to America.

So I think that if Trump turns out to be another fraudster, which we don't know yet, I think that this process of revolt will continue, because I only mentioned some elements.

I could mention that there are many countries now in realignment. For example, in the Philippines, we see Duterte. This was supposed to be the playground for the conflict with China in the South China Sea. Now Duterte sent his Defense Secretary Lorenzana to Russia and China, to buy weapons systems from Russia and China, and to establish a friendship with China; and he said, "The Philippines is no longer the colony of the U.S."

Then you have Japan, which was the junior partner of the U.S. in the Pacific. Abe went to Sochi, meeting with Putin. In three days from now, Putin will go to Japan to have a state visit. They are talking about a peace treaty between Russia and Japan.

All of these are new alignments. There is a shift in the strategic situation, and I don't think that that shift can be reversed.

Question: About Russia hacking the U.S. election. Why doesn't the U.S. have anti-hacking measures? Can you explain that?

Zepp-LaRouche: I cannot explain that, for the same reason that I cannot explain why the NSA is surveilling everyone, all their phones, their communications, worldwide. They can observe all of these things, but they don't know about terrorism. They don't know about drug-trafficking. They don't know about money-laundering. Either their system is not so good, or they are looking in the wrong direction. I can't answer your question.

Question: Will the result of the Brexit be positive for Europe, to enable continental Europe to become stronger, and to improve cooperation with the Eastern parts of Europe?

Zepp-LaRouche: I think that the EU is not functioning, and I think it is not just the Brexit. The "No" in Italy is a reflection of the same dynamic. Now you have Gentiloni, the new Prime Minister, and they will prob-

ably go for new elections. Right now, in the polls, you have the 5 Star Party leading. If they win and form the new government, they have already said that they would leave the EU and leave the Euro; and, in a certain sense, it is not functioning.

The reason I was against the introduction of the euro from the beginning, was because we said that it cannot function. You cannot have a European currency union in something which is not an optimal economic space. You cannot put advanced industry together with an agrarian country, with completely different tax laws, pension laws; and you don't want a political union, because Europe is not a people. You don't have a European people. I don't know what the Danes are saying. I don't know what is in the Danish newspapers. The people of Slovenia have no inkling of what is happening in Alsace-Lorraine, and so forth, and so on. You don't have a European people. Esperanto doesn't function. You have 28 nations, 28 histories, 28 cultures.

That doesn't mean that you can't work together. I think that the idea of Charles de Gaulle to work together as an alliance among perfectly sovereign fatherlands, that is a correct idea. And all of these fatherlands can adopt a joint mission, such as to develop Africa, or other things.

I just think that this European Union is not going to stay forever.

Question: (followup) Will it be easier for Germany and France to promote this development, as the leading countries?

Zepp-LaRouche: Everybody says that Germany is the biggest beneficiary of globalization, the EU, and the euro, but that's not really true, because if you look at it more closely, then you can say that since the introduction of the euro, the domestic market of Germany has completely stagnated. And the number of people who became poorer has increased.

Question: (followup) Regarding the dialogue with Russia.

Zepp-LaRouche: Oh yes, that would be much easier.

I do not think that this EU bureaucracy is capable of reform, because by their self-understanding they are the local pro-consuls of this empire; and I think that it would be much better if Germany, France, and other countries had individual relations. And I don't agree with this whole idea that you need a European Empire to compete with Russia and China and other emerging countries—the EU, by definition, is an empire. They have said it themselves. Robert Cooper, who has some kind of advisory function [currently serving as EU Special Adviser with regard to Myanmar], said that the EU is the fastest expanding empire in history. It's a bad idea.

And the Russians—I noticed this from the beginning of the year 2000—the Russians do not make a differentiation anymore between the EU and NATO. They said that it's the same thing. And it is the same thing.

Question: You said that the One Belt, One Road was stripped of commercial interests from the Chinese side, as opposed to the IMF, World Bank. On what basis do you say that it is less interest-driven than the Bretton Woods institutions?

Zepp-LaRouche: Well, because the question is not that I'm saying that China is perfect. I'm not saying that. But when you look at anything, you have to look at the vector of development: Is it going upward, or is it going downward? And from that standpoint, I had the advantage that I was in China in 1971, which was in the middle of the Cultural Revolution. This was so different than China today.

The Cultural Revolution was horrible for the people. The Red Guards would take people out of their homes, put them in jail, send them to the countryside, and people were distraught. And now, people in China are happy. If you talk to students, or to young people, they are optimistic. They say, "Oh, I will do this in the future. I have these plans." I talked to a group of students in Lanzhou two years ago, and they said, "We will go to Africa. We will develop Africa." I have never heard a German student say this. I did, when I was a student, but that's a long time ago.

I think that it is very worthwhile to read the speeches of Xi Jinping. There is a book, *The Governance of China*, but that only has about 60 speeches, and there are many, many more. For example, you should read the speeches he gave when he went to France, to Germany, and to India.

For example, when he went to India, he made a speech which was really incredible, because he said that he loved Indian culture from his early youth, and then he gave so many examples of the high points of Indian culture, the Gupta period, the Upanishads, the Vedic writings, Rabindranath Tagore, many predicates which prove that he really knows what he is talking about. He is not just one of these politicians who have a PR adviser about how to make nice bubbles in your speeches. You could really see that he means it. And the same for Germany. He came to Germany and he emphasized Schubert and Heine, things which I also appreciate about Germany; and he did the same thing in France.

And I don't think that the Chinese leadership would agree with me when I say this, but I think that they are less communist than Confucian. They probably would not admit that, because they are officially the Communist Party, and that's OK; but, I come from Trier, and Trier is the birthplace of Karl Marx, so I have studied Karl Marx, and I think that they are still socialist, or communist, or whatever; but they always said that they are communist with Chinese characteristics, and these Chinese characteristics are Confucianism.

And the Confucian idea of man is lifelong learning, lifelong perfection, that everyone should be a *chun tzu*, a wise man, a noble man, and Confucius said, if the government is bad, then the *chun tzu*, these wise people, should replace the government. Also the idea that you have to have an harmonious development, starting with the family, continuing in the nation, and then, larger, among the nations.

China is the only country that has not made wars of aggression, colonial wars, in its 5,000 years of history. It was invaded many times, the Opium Wars, and things like that, but China is not an aggressive nation, at all.

And if you look at what they are doing in practice,

Creative Commons

the IMF and the World Bank have prevented Third World development, and China is going from one country to the next, building science cities, helping with space cooperation, bringing in developing countries in the most advanced areas of science, in order to promote their development. I think this is a completely different approach.

I think that the Chinese have come up with a new model of government, which I have not seen in any place in Europe, the U.S., ever; and it's a model which is overcoming geopolitics, which is as if you say, "I have a win-win for cooperation. Everybody can join." Then, if everyone joins, then you have overcome geopolitics.

And geopolitics is the one thing that caused two world wars, and in the age of thermonuclear weapons, we cannot have geopolitics anymore. So I think that these are very important differences.

Sure, China has its own interests. Win-win means that China also has an interest. China has advantages, but, for example, if you ask people from Africa, "Would you rather have deals where China gets raw materials for long periods of time, but they build infrastructure for Africans?" They like that much better than Europeans who come and say, "Oh, you should obey democracy," and do nothing.

Gillesberg: Helga, would you like to make any closing remarks?

Zepp-LaRouche: I would just say that people should not just believe, or not believe, what I am saying, but take an active attitude to try to find out what the truth is, for themselves. Because the world is not helped by replacing one ideology by another. The only way you can be certain, is that you become a truth-seeking person yourself. Because the whole question about what went wrong, is that people forgot what it is to be an honest truth-seeking person, taking the truth not as something you reach finally, but something you always improve.

Schiller had a beautiful writing about universal history, where he said that the philosophical mind is the first one to take his own system apart, to put it together more perfectly again.

Two days ago in Berlin, we had a very important event, which was also about the dialogue of cultures, and a very important presentation, which you can soon see on our webpage, by a double-bass player who spoke about the importance of Wilhelm Furtwängler as a conductor; and he gave some musical examples, and he compared the performances of Furtwängler with some modern conductors, and the difference is so unbelievable. The music of Furtwängler is transparent. It is beautiful. It is absolutely overwhelmingly uplifting; and many of the other conductors are just playing along, with no respect for what the composition is.

And he really described, with many quotes from Furtwängler, that what is needed is this inner quality of truthfulness. That you don't fake it, because if you're not truthful—for example, you cannot recite poetry, if you're not truthful. You cannot sing beautifully, if you're not truthful. Sure, you can sing brilliantly, you can do all kinds of tricks, and it impresses people, but to really produce art, you have to be truthful. You have to try to understand the poetical idea, the musical idea. You have to step back with your ego, behind what the composer or the poet wrote. And that's what is wrong with modern theater. In Regietheater, they just say, "I don't care what Schiller wrote, or what Shakespeare wrote. I just make my modern interpretation. I can put Harley Davidsons into Shakespeare, and it doesn't matter." And that is not art.

And I think the question is, "What do you do with your life?" That is really the question. Are you becoming a creative person, devoted to that with your life, that you contribute to enable mankind to move on a little step further, and become better.

Or, are you just eating three tons of caviar, and owning 3,000 Porsches. And then, when you die, they write on your gravestone, "He/she ate three tons of caviar, and had 3,000 Porsches," and that was it.

No, you should try to be an honest person, trying to make human society better with what you do. And, once you do that, you become happy. Then you are free. This inner freedom, is what you should try to find. And that is the only way that we will win this battle. It's not Trump. It is, can we get enough people to be innerly free.

And then we win.

I. Manhattan Leads Mankind Upwards

MANHATTAN PROJECT DIALOGUE

The Strength To Create A Cultural Renaissance

Excerpts from the Dec. 17 Manhattan Project in Dialogue, with Helga Zepp-LaRouche and Megan Beets.

Dennis Speed: On behalf of the LaRouche Political Action Committee I'd like to welcome everybody here today. My name is Dennis Speed. And despite the various forms of scare tactics underway, including around this meeting, we're going ahead.

Some of you know that we're involved in another event which is going to happen a little later today; many of our members at least are involved in an event that involves a concert that will be happening in the evening. But you also know that we have a certain context in which we're operating; and that context is not defined by the peculiar and sometimes insane actions of certain heads of state. For example, Barack Obama and his recent claims about Russia. It's really defined by something much larger. I just want to refer here to a statement made by Dr. Martin Luther King. It's not well known; it's contained in one of the sermons that he gave called "Strength to Love." It's not the entire statement, but it's the most element of the statement. He said:

> Man can think a poem and write it. He can think a symphony and compose it. He can think of a great civilization and produce it. ... He can be a Handel moving into the highest heavens and

LPACTV

Helga Zepp-LaRouche

transcribing the glad thunders and gentle sightings of the great Messiah. By his ability to reason, by his power and memory and his gift of imagination, man transcends time and space. As marvelous as are the stars, as great as is Handel's *Messiah,* is the mind of the man that studies them.

That statement pretty well summarizes, I think, the actual orientation we take to what people often call "politics." Many years ago, Lyndon LaRouche wrote an article called "Politics as Art" in which he talked about this, but we've asked—I've asked—that Helga LaRouche address us today as we go into that later event from the standpoint that there's a need that Americans have to consider a completely new, if you will, cultural and intellectual platform for their behavior in politics. She has worked for over 30 years to get this point across to Americans, and I thought it was an important point to be made to all of us prior to those activities. It's always my honor to present Helga LaRouche; and we will hopefully have some time for questions and answers. So, Helga?

Our Dangerous Situation

Helga Zepp-LaRouche: Yes, hello; good day. I think everybody is in a state of enormous tension, because the world is not in a safe place yet. I watched

Prof. Stephen Cohen of Princeton (right) sees the charges against Russia as an attack on Trump's plan for a policy of détente with Russia.

yesterday the live press conference, supposedly the last press conference of President Obama, and what he said there was really incredibly evil. Because he claims that they have evidence—no, he didn't even claim that; they said that Russia had hacked the DNC's and other computers and interfered with the election process in the United States. Up to the present moment, there has not been any evidence presented. Then he threatened actions against Russia in retaliation; both obviously open, but also hidden, but that Russia would find out what the message was.

That is a rather unveiled threat; and there is a real hysteria on the side of those people who lost the election. Hillary today came out and said basically that Putin's interference was his personal revenge, because Putin didn't like what she did as Secretary of State. It needs to be stressed that a very respectable group, the Veteran Intelligence Professionals for Sanity (VIPS), including such people as Senator Mike Gravel and Ray McGovern, put out a statement that their long years of experience as cyber security experts caused them to look at these emails, and that they have no doubt that these were not hacks, but leaks like the kind of leaks Edward Snowden and Chelsea Manning had done from the inside. Anyway, there is a big hype, and I think we should be very aware that this is very dangerous.

A confrontation with Russia, with China, is the other thing that could happen between now and President-elect Trump actually taking office. The recent de-

velopments in the South China Sea speak to that. We are not in a safe world by any means. The hysteria about the so-called "fall" of Aleppo, as it is being characterized by the media, is not less. Here you have a military solution to a problem which it was obviously not possible to solve politically; among other things, because of the sabotage by the United States of the talks in Geneva. So, the military option was the only remaining one; and now people are liberated. People should be happy that ISIS has been suffering a terrible defeat. I am pointing out that this incredible spinning of events shows you that we are not in a safe situation by any means.

In the United States, but also in Europe, people can almost be separated into two groups: First, those who have not yet recovered from the so-called "shock" of the Trump election. These are the people who believe in geopolitics, in globalization—people who believe in the present system, which has brought the world to this point. Then you have those who are very happy that Trump won; they hope that he will stick it to Wall Street. But we have to see whether he will do it, given his Goldman-Sachs appointments. And we have to see whether he will stick it to the establishment in general.

I reference these circumstances very briefly, because I don't think that either of those mindsets—neither the people who are freaked out about Hillary losing, nor those who say that Trump will stick it to the establishment—is adequate. We have to introduce a completely different level of thinking into the political process, which is why the performance of the *Messiah* and a long series of other concerts is so extremely important. We have discussed this many times, but I will say it again. Why is Classical art and Classical music in particular so absolutely crucial if mankind is going to get out of this crisis?

Why Are We So Stupid?

The problem is, and I think most of you agree, that for many years—almost 50 years since the assassination of John F. Kennedy and the cover-up of his murder—the paradigm of the Western world and especially the United States has led to an incredible brutalization of the population. And many people are not happy about the future. Life expectancy in the United States is going down for the first time in a very long time; there is simply no better indicator for living standards and well-being of a people than life expectancy. If life expectancy goes down in a civilized nation, that is a sure proof it is in a full crisis and in decay.

Now, how do we get people out of this? How do we get people to be their more noble selves? How do you get people to a more elevated level of thinking than just saying, "Let's hope

EIRNS/Don Clark

Schiller Institute performance of Mozart's Requiem in Manhattan on Sept. 10, 2016.

Trump will stick it to them"? Because that is still an emotion of anger, frustration and so forth. The problem is, we have discussed in these meetings many times that the oligarchy rules over society by reducing people to beings of just feelings, emotions; and they are very good at manipulating these emotions. That people are angry; that people are depressed; that people have rage; that people have joy in decadent pleasures. All of these are tools of the oligarchy. When man is on that level, he is not truly human.

The first thinker who really described this very effectively was Plato in his famous cave allegory. He said the people who only believe in their emotions are like those who sit in a cave where they see only dimly-lit shadows of events which take place outside of the cave; and they take these shadows for the real thing. People who only believe in sense certainty, they have different forms. For example, monetarism is one such form of believing in the senses. Or utilitarianism, that only what is useful is valid. Or nominalism, positivism. There are all these varieties of "isms," but they basically mean that people are not really thinking.

Freedom to Know Truth

Great Classical art opens the way to understanding real principles, those principles which are behind the

sensuous appearance. And it enables one to learn how to become truly free. That is a quality which has been a very rare commodity in these periods. That people really have inner freedom; that they have their own judgement; that they develop their inner voice; that they learn to listen to their inner voice—you can also call it conscience.

It is generally great art which allows people to develop that quality in a playful way. Because when you are looking or listening to great art, this is not the seriousness of real life; this is like the existential in that sense. But you can study the process of creativity in a playful way. I think it is extremely important that we not forget that mankind must make the jump to a completely new paradigm, in which we are not just thinking about one nation. Trump has promised "America first." Well, that may be a good antidote to what has happened with this so-called globalization up until now. But what is required is a completely different thinking, which is why I like Friedrich Schiller so very much. And why I think his ideas provide such a richness of concepts that we need to get to the New Paradigm.

Schiller, for example, said it is not a contradiction to be a patriot and a world citizen; I think we have reached a state in human history in which we must establish that no nation can express a self interest if it is in contradiction to the goals of humanity as a whole. Therefore, this quality of becoming a world citizen while loving your nation without contradiction is something we have to introduce into this debate. Only then can the American people join in the New Paradigm of the New Silk Road for common goals of humanity—for the community of destiny for the future of mankind, as Xi Jinping always describes it.

I think that Schiller is very important for another reason, and that is that he—under the terrible collapse of the French Revolution leading to the Jacobin terror, the killing of people through the guillotine—he was completely appalled. Schiller, in reaction to this Terror and associated developments in France, wrote the *Aesthetical Letters*; where he basically said that the only way you can have an improvement in the political life is through the ennoblement of the individual. Now, I know that that is not exactly what people think about politics; and they don't think about—the only way mankind moves forward, is that each of us; you, me, everybody ennobles themselves or tries to do so throughout their entire life. I think the idea of mankind which Schiller developed, is the notion of the beautiful soul; because I think that it's the key to a lot of things.

Crucial Role of Our Inner Freedom

Schiller's idea of the beautiful soul is the soul of a person for whom freedom and necessity, passion and duty, are one. I think this is a concept one has to think about, because freedom and necessity—what does it mean? It means that, no matter what the circumstances of your life are, you do what is necessary, not only for yourself and your family, but for mankind as a whole—which may have different shapes and different requirements at different times.

Right now, it means to bring the United States into the paradigm with the rest of the world and overcome this terrible danger of a confrontation with Russia and China, which would surely mean the extinction of civilization.

Now, what does it mean to find your freedom in what is necessary? I want you to think about it, because most people have not thought about it, and it is the key to being truly free. Freedom does not just mean the absence of chains and the absence of constraints. It means that you are completely a self-deter-

Friedrich Schiller

mining person, and that at the same time, you do your duty with passion. You are not a Kantian who says, "Oh, I have to do my duty and therefore I'm truly sour; but I'm a moral person and I'm doing what I'm supposed to." You see many such people, but you have to joyfully do what is necessary. That requires the education of your emotions so that, as Schiller demands, you can always trust them blindly, because your impulses will never tell you anything different than what Reason would command.

That is a high standard, but I think it is absolutely possible to accomplish it. It is great Classical art which is the field where you can rehearse what this requires. Schiller, in the very interesting piece of drama which he wrote which used a Classical Greek example, namely *The Bride of Messina*, he wrote an introduction where he discusses the function and the power of great art. He says when people listen to a great piece of art—in that case, he talked about the Greek chorus; not the musical chorus, the chorus in the Greek drama. He said that when people are exposed to this, it sets a power free inside them—a power which sets people truly free, internally free. And that freedom remains even when the performance is over.

Limitations of Trump's Entourage

Some of you have experienced that already, during the great celebrations on the 15th anniversary of September 11th, with the performances we had in four churches in New York. Obviously, this is a very precious gift which we have to really fight to make the more dominant culture. I'm perfectly happy to give the President-elect a lot of credit that he will do interesting things; at least half of what he has posed will come true, namely renewing the relationship with Russia and China and putting it on a good basis. And that would be gigantic.

But I have the most severe doubts that this question of a Classical education and the aesthetical improvement of man can be expected from this Trump administration. But it is the absolute necessary requirement to make America great again; which he has promised. I think you need a kind of spirit of ennoblement, of the sublime; and that level you do not find in any of the utterances from the Trump side. At least, I haven't heard anything even close to that. But you have heard it from such people as Benjamin Franklin, as George Washington, as Alexander Hamilton, John Quincy Adams, and especially Lincoln. If you think about the Gettysburg Address, and the beautiful spirit which is expressed in that, that is the mindset—not in the predicates, but in the spirit—which people should be at all times if they are truly free.

So, in that sense, I think we have a tremendous chance over this Christmas period and the holiday season—people always have some time to read, to think, to listen to music. I would encourage you to do not just the things you usually do in this season, such as going to the mall and buying gifts for people. All that is fine, but the real meaning of this season is to find for yourself and find the higher identity which we have to mobilize to get the world into a safer place. So, that's really all I wanted to address, and that's what my remarks to you are at this moment. [applause]

Questions and Answers

Q: Good afternoon. How are you? This is Jessica from Brooklyn. First I wanted to say that I'm very glad that we're having this meeting. I was a little worried about attendance; people coming with the snow and rain and this and that. It's a little earlier time, but I see that we have a nice group of people here; and I'm glad

Painting of Lincoln by George Peter Alexander Healy (1869).

to be here, and I'm really happy that you are addressing us and changing the way we're thinking about going forward with making what we want to happen really happen. With this situation Obama did the other day, yesterday, his speech and all that; I saw that. I just wanted to say that, first of all, that I'm very happy that you're here addressing us; and I think everyone in this room is.

My question is not so much an actual question, but I'm a teacher and I'm seeing a lot of different things happening in my school and in my union. People, like you said, are tense; there's some hysteria going on. There's a lot of stuff happening. Would you comment please on what you feel a Classical education is. In many different ways, we can talk about education; we can talk about the actual subjects, the intent of what education should bring about. I've been thinking about that in watching other people—my parents, my fellow teachers. So, if you could please comment on what you feel we should be doing, or what should be meant by a Classical education?

Education of Individual Character

Zepp-LaRouche: Obviously, my husband Lyn is somebody who has developed that method in many ways. There is a great reference in Germany, which has—apart from my husband—developed the best education system I know of, and that's Wilhelm von Humboldt. Not only did he design the German education system and university system, but in the 19th Century, there was not one professor in the United States who was not either educated by this method or by somebody who had studied it in Germany. The influence of Humboldt in the 19th Century in the United States was tremendous.

The reason I think he is still extremely important today, maybe more than ever before, is that he defined as the goal of education not any particular skill. He said if you learn how to learn, you can improve your skills throughout your life. What he defined as the goal of education is the beauty of the character. I don't know of any school today that has a goal that the end result of the pupils going to the school should be that they have beautiful characters. But if you look at the violence, the meanness, the brutality, all of the behaviors people retain—especially in the schools, where many teachers are afraid of their pupils; this is a common phenomenon these days. The idea that the end goal should be a beautiful character, I think is more important than at any time before.

Schiller was a close friend of Humboldt, and shared these ideas, but Humboldt had a very clear idea of how you reach that goal. He said that there are certain subjects which are more suited than others to have this effect of developing all of the potentialities that are in a young person into a harmonious totality. He said, first of all, you have to have a command over your own language in its highest expressions.

Wilhelm von Humboldt

Obviously the highest expressions of your own language are the most beautiful Classical poets, because they can express concepts which you just do not find in prose. There is a big difference between lyrics and poetry, and prose; because lyrics and poetry force the mind to access those higher levels where new concepts are formed. Naturally, you cannot think what you cannot express in words; and therefore, the study of the best examples of poetry is the key to all other subjects. If you don't have the language,— Britney Spears once proudly said that she has a vocabulary of only 80 words. That obviously limits the amount of what she can think.

Humboldt then also said, you have to study universal history, because only if you are able to place your own identity and your own life in the context, not only of the history of your nation, but in the history of universal mankind, can you find the right place. Schiller expressed that you have to connect your dwindling existence, which is short because people live a very short time, to the long chain of generations before you and generations after you. And that is what gives you your identity; it makes you grateful to the generations before you and gives you a vision of what you have to contribute to make better generations after you possible. Then, naturally, come geography, music, natural sciences, other languages.

PlayStation or Humboldt?

So I think to really go with the Humboldt conception and to reintroduce Humboldt would be such an extremely important start because it is not just science, it is not just art as such, but it is the combination, the two things absolutely have to go together. Because scientists and artists are the only two professions, so to speak, that believe in universal principles. Natural science—physics, biology, chemistry—these are areas in which, if you make an adequate experiment, you can repeat it anywhere around the globe. If you find a discovery in the United States and if it's a true physical principle, any Chinese or any African can repeat it in Africa, or in Luxembourg, or in some other place, because it's a universal principle.

And the same goes for great Classical art, but especially music, which is why you find in orchestras, people from all over the world working together, performing a concert, and you don't even notice that they come from different countries and cultures, because they have one universal language.

So science and music in particular are really important, because they free you from opinion, they free you from the liberal notion that "my opinion is as good as yours," which is commonplace now. People don't accept the idea that there is truth and that you have to be truthful; people say, "it doesn't matter, what *I* think is as good as what *you* say, and therefore, there is no criterion for truth at all," which obviously prevents people from finding this key I'm talking about.

The future paradigm will mean that people think like creative scientists; that's why Lyn puts such an emphasis on individuals such as Vernadsky and Einstein. And naturally, thinking like Beethoven, thinking like Mozart, or Handel for that matter, that is what truth is; that's how you can find truth. And I think for the children today who are *so*—you know, the children today have almost no chance, because if they look at TV, if they play games using PlayStation, they have no chance to have this love for truth. So I think that would be the most important to accomplish, because once you accomplish that, they start to seek truth and become truth-seeking people, and then it's the key for everything.

The Great Poet of the United States

Speed: When you were talking about Lincoln, I was thinking about his First Inaugural Address, which has this phrase at the end that has become very famous:

Oil on canvas, 1949, by A.E. Yeletsky

Portrait of V.I. Vernadsky of the Russian Academy of Sciences, Moscow, hanging in the Institute of Geochemistry and Analytical Chemistry named after him.

"The mystic chords of memory, stretching from every battlefield and patriot grave to every living heart and hearthstone all over this broad land, will yet swell the chorus of the Union, when again touched, as surely they will be, by the better angels of our nature."

I remember, this must be back in 1986, at a conference where some of us of the Schiller Institute were, you made the point that the great poet of the United States is Abraham Lincoln. And you also referenced it earlier, and in your conclusion to us, I just want to ask you—if you would—to tell us why you say that, why you think that, and how you think we might be able to use the example of Lincoln, particularly now with this new Presidency, and this new opportunity?

What a Republic Requires

Zepp-LaRouche: It is because Lincoln has this quality of noble thinking. And if you study what he said at various points, you find that quality. And in a certain sense, it is this idea too, which is expressed in the Gettysburg Address, in particular, that you cannot just think for the moment: You have to connect your personal life with what others have contributed—you can live the way you live because of all your ancestry, and you have the idea that you, with your life, contribute something so that mankind is richer when you are no longer here, because of what you have done.

That quality, which is sort of a Good Samaritan impulse,— that is what Schiller called the Good Samaritan, who does the good without thinking what advantage he may have, or what's in it for him; none of these thoughts enter your thinking. And at the same time, you have a vision for the future, and Lincoln surely had that. So in one sense, he may have been the greatest President of the United States, and he is the measurement for any President from now on.

So all of you should think like that: Because a republic only functions when everyone takes the same kind of responsibility as the President, and a republic only functions when you have a sufficient number of people who also demand of themselves that they qualify themselves so that they *could* become President! You should study economics, foreign policy, science, art, so that if for some reason, you would have to be President, you could do it. And then you have a functioning republic—if many, many people are thinking like that, even if they don't become President. That's the way to look at the world and to look at your nation. [applause]

Speed: That's certainly a worthwhile task for the Manhattan Project to take up, it's a good way for people think about what we've got to do today as well.

Thank you very much Helga, and you'll be getting a report some time tomorrow morning on our work with the *Messiah* down in Brooklyn.

Unite To Spread Noesis Beyond Mars

Megan Beets: Those of us alive today are presented with an incredible opportunity, which is the opportunity, though not the guarantee, of leaving for the next 50, 100, perhaps thousands of years ahead, a new paradigm, which has never existed among mankind before, a new system established based on the true nature of mankind. And you think about the implications of that, that means that the empire system is *over forever*, relegated to a past and long-dead, never-to-return era of mankind. This is a very challenging idea. It's a very big idea. And it's one that those of us assembled here, and everywhere, should take up as our mission, for the rest of the time allotted to us on this planet.

Now that opportunity presented us, to establish a new paradigm, obviously comes with a great responsibility, and I want to go back to the quote from Martin Luther King that Dennis read at the opening. He said that "Mankind can think of a great civilization and produce it." So, upon what principles do you base that civilization? What is the most truthful notion of the nature of mankind that we can strive for, upon which we will be confident in establishing this new paradigm?

The human mind is a completely unique form of existence, on this planet, and anywhere else in this Universe, as far as we are aware. Human beings are a form of life which can study the Universe, which can confront paradoxes, which can confront problems which challenge our knowledge, and which can imagine solutions, which can imagine notions of a principle which is generating the kind of paradoxical effect we see in the Universe. We can imagine solutions to scientific problems, and generate them from the human mind, and these notions are so true, that they allow human beings to exert a greater power over nature than we had before. That's an incredible form of existence.

As an example of what I'm referring to, we've never seen an atom. We've certainly never seen the nucleus of an atom; no microscope can image for us, the nucleus of an atom. And yet, our vision of the organization of the atomic nucleus is so close to nature, that with this notion, with this idea, we are able to split the atom; we're able to fuse atomic nuclei to create new elements; we're able to create fusion plasmas, manufacturing new elements, breaking down current materials, and exerting a finely tuned control over nature, that allows us to first of all, unleash enormous amounts of power and energy, to generate electricity, to generate explosions for infrastructure construction; but also allows us to fine-tune materials like steel, to create steels that are stronger than anything we could have produced from purely natural elements.

The most inspiring notion that's given us the most inspiring power over nature, up to this point, for me, is Johannes Kepler's poetic notion of the planetary orbits; his poetic notion of the Solar system. Because that has allowed *us*, to create artificial orbits, intentionally, to put satellites into orbit and to put mankind into orbit. And for me, it's mankind's potential to leave this planet and bring that process of creativity to other bodies of the Solar system, to begin improving them, bringing them to a higher state of organization than ever before; giving them a new meaning in the Solar system, something they could not have had without the presence of creative life, in the form of human beings. To me, that's the most inspiring power over nature that we've achieved up to this point, and it absolutely defines something which *is* the common aims of mankind.

Mankind on this planet must unite in our scientific capabilities, our scientific insight, and our economic power to get mankind *off* of the planet, out onto the Moon and to Mars beyond—and we'll see when we can get beyond that. We must come together to establish this new era of mankind.

A New Cultural Platform for The Post-Obama Era

by Dennis Speed

For we wrestle not against flesh and blood, but against principalities, against powers, against the rulers of the darkness of this world, against spiritual wickedness in high places.
—St. Paul, Ephesians 6:12

Dec. 20—The 700-plus people that gathered at St. Joseph's Co-Cathedral on Dec. 17, 2016 for the "Holiday Unity Concert" sponsored by the "Foundation for the Revival of Classical Culture," responded both to the idea and the execution of this latest in a series of "experiments with truth" being conducted in the context of the evolution of Lyndon LaRouche's Manhattan Project. Helga Zepp-LaRouche, the founder and head of the Schiller Institute, in a presentation made the afternoon prior to the evening musical performance by the Schiller Institute New York Community Chorus and the New England Symphonic Ensemble, stressed the strategic and moral necessity of such events: "I think we have to introduce a completely different level of thinking into the political process, which is why the performance of the *Messiah* and a long series of other concerts is so important."

A new cultural platform, capable of advancing and sustaining the highest conceptions of man and nature, must immediately be built as the underpinning for a new form of intellectual practice in the American republic. This is not something that the incoming Trump administration, nor, certainly, the outgoing Obama non-administration could provide. This very quality, however, of intellectual insight, as practiced, for example, by Albert Einstein, is the only sure road to durable survival past the immediate threat of thermonuclear war.

Now that, even for the gullible, it has become clear with the completion of the Electoral College vote that Donald Trump is indeed the President-Elect of the United States, for a moment it might be worthwhile for all involved to consider how America could have sunk to such a low intellectual level, as to be convinced for even a moment of the truthfulness of any of the assertions made by Hillary Clinton, or Barack Obama, or his British masters, on any issues of any importance. To understand how our nation, and many of our people, have sunk to such an intellectual nadir, a little history—a shock to the soul—is required.

It is little appreciated that almost every writer, painter, playwright, and poet in the United States in the post-World War Two period, from 1947 until the mid-1960s, was financed, sometimes unknowingly, by a British Intelligence and "CIA" outfit called the "Congress for Cultural Freedom" (CCF). Classical culture, particularly as that was or might be associated with

Attendees at the Dec. 17 Holiday Unity Conference in Brooklyn, N.Y.

Germany, was to be replaced with "home-grown, authentic, democratic American popular culture," much of it created by intelligence agencies or their employees like Jackson Pollock, Sidney Hook, or media-promoted pseudo-persons like Timothy Leary of 1960s LSD fame. The children of persons involved with, or employed by, the intelligence services of the U.S. Army and Navy, including persons employed at facilities like Fort Detrick, were used as guinea pigs in LSD experiments in the 1950s, 60s, and 70s, as has been documented in various locations.

From its first intervention at the Waldorf Astoria Hotel in 1949, at a time when Bertrand Russell and others were actively considering dropping nuclear bombs on Russia, the Congress for Cultural Freedom hovered around New York City, the intellectual capital of the United States. The McCarthyism of the 1950s drove the sons and daughters both of those persecuted, and of those intimidated by the persecution, into the ranks of what would somewhat later be given the name of the "counter-culture," later to be known as the "rock-drug-sex counterculture." The forms of so-called musical practice and tastes which are said to predominate in present-day America, are largely a product of those earlier actions by the CCF.

Educating One's Emotions

Helga Zepp-LaRouche clinically diagnosed this pathology, but from the higher standpoint of a solution-concept:

We have discussed this many times, but let me say it again. Why is Classical art and Classical music in particular so absolutely crucial if mankind is going to get out of this crisis? The problem is—and I think that most of you agree with me—that for many years, more than fifty years since the assassination of John F. Kennedy and the cover-up of his murder, the paradigm of the Western world and especially the United States has really led to an incredible brutalization of the population. Many people are still not happy about the future....

Now, how do people get out of this? How do we get people to be their more noble selves? How do you get people to be more elevated than just saying, 'Let's hope Trump will stick it to them'? [Or, it must be added, to be more rational than the emotionally unstable supporters of Obama puppet and subordinate, Hillary Clinton?] Because there is still an emotion of anger and frustration. The problem is, we have discussed in these meetings many times that the oligarchy rules over society by reducing people to beings of just feelings, emotions; and they are very good at manipulating these emotions. That people are angry; that people are depressed; that people have rage; that people have joy in decadent pleasures. All these [feelings] are tools of the oligarchy. When man is on that level, he is not truly human....

Now what great Classical art does, is it shows a way that people can first of all learn to understand real principles; those principles which are behind the sensuous appearance. And they can learn how to become truly free.

To achieve this, a new process of organizing is therefore taking shape in New York City, in the LaRouche "Manhattan Project," in this phase to be largely guided by the insights of Helga Zepp-LaRouche into the work of the great German "Poet of Freedom," Friedrich Schiller. Instead of merely political program, policy, and tactics, this new movement starts from the standpoint of improving the character of the American people, to qualify them to each become both patriots of their nations, and world-citizens at the same time. This was the original purpose of education, as conceived by Wilhelm von Humboldt and other German thinkers. It used to be the standard for education in the United States, until the late 19th Century. It is now being reintroduced into currency in America through the "choral process," also termed "the Manhattan Project."

The working relationship between freedom, education, and art is the domain of the new cultural platform that must be established, starting in New York City, where the Presidential transition is presently occurring, and where the "dialogue of world civilizations" on matters of this type is most capable of taking place at this time on the planet as a whole. Wilhelm von Humboldt, the founder of Humboldt University in Berlin, a central figure in the philosophy of education and one of Schiller's closest associates, points out that, "Whatever does not spring from a man's free choice, or is only the result of instruction and guidance, does not enter into his very being, but still remains alien to his true nature; he does not perform it with truly human energies, but merely with mechanical exactness."

The Schiller Institute/Guy Alberghini

The chorus at the Dec. 17 concert.

Helga Zepp-LaRouche admonished her audience that it would be the unique task of those associated with Lyndon LaRouche and his method of discovery, to provide the means for the United States to successfully adapt a new cultural platform that would enable America to enter into principled alliance with China, Russia, India, and other nations, in pursuit of the goal of "making America great again." Alexander Hamilton's example, of fighting for freedom as a revolutionary, through his economics, and his dedication to preserving and extending that freedom to all Americans, enslaved and free, and to their posterity, is what is being studied by Schiller Institute members in the form of Lyndon LaRouche's "Four Laws" each week.

Ennobling the Culture

The 750-plus person audience at the St. Joseph's concert in Brooklyn, New York was brought there by unusual means. No "advertising" was done for the event by radio, newspaper, or even email. All word of the concert was spread through the church and by volunteer organizers.

Several people, when asked how they knew about the concert, replied "it was everywhere"! Several small businesses displayed posters, some institutions took additional leaflets, and other events were leafleted prior to the concert itself. One woman, the owner of an Italian restaurant, told organizers of how she had watched the church, which has been recently renovated, go from being in a dilapidated condition to a thing of real beauty. She became particularly enthusiastic upon learning that

a chorus existed in Brooklyn, and that she could join it. Musicians were discovered in dentists' offices and other establishments—people who had a love for music, but who due to circumstances were unable to pursue music as a career.

Monsignor Harrington, in his welcome to the participants in the concert, commented that the present, so-called popular culture, focuses on debasing people rather than ennobling them. He referenced that the idea of the Schiller Institute was precisely the opposite. The concert itself demonstrated the truthfulness of his statement.

Lynn Yen, founder of the sponsoring Foundation for the Revival of Classical Culture, spoke following Monsignor Harrington. In her remarks, she said, "In a far more divided America than we today inhabit, Abraham Lincoln concluded his First Inaugural Address of 1861 with a musical idea of a new national harmony: 'The mystic chords of memory, stretching from every battlefield and patriot grave to every living heart and hearthstone all over this broad land, will yet swell the chorus of the Union, when again touched, as surely they will be, by the better angels of our nature.' We of the Foundation for the Revival of Classical Culture intend to create that chorus of unity right here in Brooklyn. The chorus will not be partisan. The sopranos will not just sing out on their own behalf, and drown out the altos. The basses will not protest against the tenors. The chorus will not pit one group of people against another. The chorus will not appeal to an electoral college to select its conductor. The chorus will not put up walls.

The chorus will not shout, it will not scream. The chorus will sing. The chorus will deliver a message of Beauty and Truth, through singing."

A Scientifically Literate Population

While there were many moments of profound and deep reflection during the evening, the alto/soprano duet, "And He Shall Feed His Flock," from Handel's *Messiah,* sung by Patrice Eaton and Theresa Cincione, was an *unheimlich* moment in the concert, in which singers, orchestra, and audience were momentarily as one. Conductor John Sigerson's approach to the piece's musical direction made this moment possible. The extent of his study of and control over the performance of the music was particularly seen in a recitative for tenor from Bach's Cantata #140, *Wachet Auf.* Because the designated tenor soloist was not available, Sigerson was required to turn to the audience and sing the part himself, much to the surprise, delight, and satisfaction of all present.

The two choral settings of African-American spirituals were conducted by Diane Sare, the founder of the Schiller Institute New York Community Chorus. These spirituals—"Behold the Star" (with soloists Scott Mooney, tenor, and Michelle Fuchs, soprano), and "Sister Mary Had-a But One Child" (with Christopher Sare, tenor, and Costas Tsourakis, bass-baritone)— were virtually unknown to the audience, although the songs themselves may have been familiar. Arranged by William Dawson, one of the foremost living authorities on the African-American spiritual, "Behold A Star," the first selection introducing the concert, riveted the attention of the audience. That attention, essentially, never wavered from the concert's beginning. The soloists— Ziwen Xiang, tenor, Jay Baylon, bass-baritone, Theresa Cincione, and Patrice Eaton—were greeted with enthusiastic applause after each of their various arias, particularly in the *Messiah.*

Each of the upcoming concert programs and other cultural events now being contemplated by the churches of Brooklyn, the Foundation for the Revival of Classical Culture, and the Schiller Institute, is to be embedded within a successive overall program, forming a single process.

This process consists of the organizing of a 1,500-

The Schiller Institute/Guy Alberghini

Chorus director John Sigerson singing recitative for tenor in Bach's Cantata No. 140, Wachet Auf.

person citywide chorus, composed primarily of non-professional singers who will become trained in Bel Canto singing methods at the proper tuning of middle C equal to 256 vibrations per second (C=256). (This tuning is often referred to as the "Verdi pitch," because of that composer's fierce advocacy of A=432 as a standard for proper vocal performance.) This will include a chorus devoted completely to performing African-American spirituals as a specialty (though not exclusively), as well as a dedicated youth chorus, in addition to the now regularly-performing adult chorus. Elements of this program presently exist in Brooklyn, Manhattan, Queens, and the Bronx. The purpose is to establish a scientifically literate population once again in the United States. That scientific literacy, however, must begin from Albert Einstein's standpoint—and that means, from the standpoint of a deep appreciation and practice of classical musical performance, appreciation, and even composition. Einstein's love for Mozart, and his deep commitment to music as a classical mode of thinking, underscored everything that he accomplished in science.

The Presidential transition must be accompanied by our population's own transition from post-9/11 Bush/Obama subjects, British-style, to a once again thinking citizenry, American-style. Classical music's revival as the primary means of a new public discourse with the world—as that world is present in the very population of New York City—is the "cultural geodesic" by means of which we may yet be permitted to bring about the greatest uplift in the history of humanity, despite the damage done by the CCF's British-originated "rock-drug-sex counter culture."

STRATEGIC DEFENSE OF EARTH

A New Paradigm for Russia, China, America, and All Mankind

The following are edited excerpts from the LaRouche PAC's weekly Webcast of Dec. 16, featuring Benjamin Deniston of the LaRouche PAC Science Team.

In the recent weeks, we've had some discussions with Lyndon LaRouche about the prospect of bringing the principle of the SDI—the Strategic Defense Initiative, or in its modern form, the Strategic Defense of Earth (SDE)—bringing that principle back onto the table in this potential new strategic environment where, assuming Obama doesn't start thermonuclear war before the next President even has a chance to take power, we could see a new alliance emerging between the United States, Russia, and China. Mr. LaRouche was very supportive of this being a time in which the Strategic Defense of Earth policy can come back as a real pillar of a new security architecture for the planet. This can be a critical pillar for how the security, the defense and the military institutions of nations in this new era might come together, with cooperation on the new challenges, the common threats and issues that face all nations.

The reason why I say this is a principle, is because we're in a new—really for the past couple of generations—a new historical phase for mankind in this thermonuclear age. We've reached the point where if we continue a geopolitical, imperial policy,

EIRNS/Stuart Lewis
LaRouche continues the fight for his antiballistic-missile defense policy at a conference in Washington, D.C. on April 13, 1983.

where a leading power tries to maintain control at all costs, this could lead to full-scale war, as it has in past periods, past centuries, but this time you would be talking about the annihilation of mankind. In this thermonuclear age, full-blown warfare has the ability to wipe out civilization as we know it.

Now, however, we are seeing the potential for a build-up around that kind of war to be put off the table, to be put on the back burner by a new administration. Instead, what we are talking about, with this Strategic Defense of Earth, is a cooperative effort for the broader exploration of space, the joint development of space. This needs to become a central positive issue that we rally nations around; it can't just become, "Let's not have war or conflict because it's bad"; but, "Let's have a positive, truthful conception—a real principle—of the issues that face all nations together, that we should be rallying around in cooperation."

That outlook was the original intent of LaRouche's SDI: *LaRouche's SDI,* not necessarily the program that got implemented to some degree. LaRouche's idea of the SDI, was a joint open cooperative program with the Soviet Union, sharing technologies and capabilities and jointly developing new capabilities to—as Ronald Reagan said—"render the threat of thermonuclear weapons impotent and obsolete." We would actually be working with the Soviets to do this, and Mr. LaRouche recruited Dr. Edward Teller and President Reagan around this idea.

These were not hippie, flower-wielding peaceniks; these were not people that just ran around saying, "No war. War is bad." These were pretty serious, staunch conservatives—Cold Warriors to a certain degree—but they recognized the truthful validity of what LaRouche was developing around his idea of the SDI. Mankind had reached a point where we needed positive, collaborative, joint development of these kinds of capabilities for the common aims of nations. Mr. LaRouche came incredibly close, in collaboration with Reagan, Teller, and others, to really overturning the strategic framework back in the '80s with that program.

This outlook has not really gone away. We have discussed this on shows in the past, but it's worth just reminding people that in the '90s, in the aftermath of the attempt to get the full SDI program, there was a re-emergence of the same idea around the defense of Earth. There was a recognition at that time—in the early '90s—that the Earth is actually incredibly vulnerable to asteroid strikes and comet strikes; and we should actually be looking at what we can do to defend the planet from these kinds of potential disasters. That was something that Dr. Edward Teller, in direct collaboration with other veterans of the SDI and their direct counterparts in Russia, took up as a major focus in the '90s. There was a whole series of conferences, investigations and proposals for the same type of joint, open cooperation between the defense institutions and related institutions in the United States and Russia, for cooperation around this common threat through the defense of Earth from not only missiles, but missiles coming from the Solar system—these asteroids. Unfortunately, it didn't fully go through at the time. Instead, we had the continuation of this geopolitical framework, which has obviously continued through

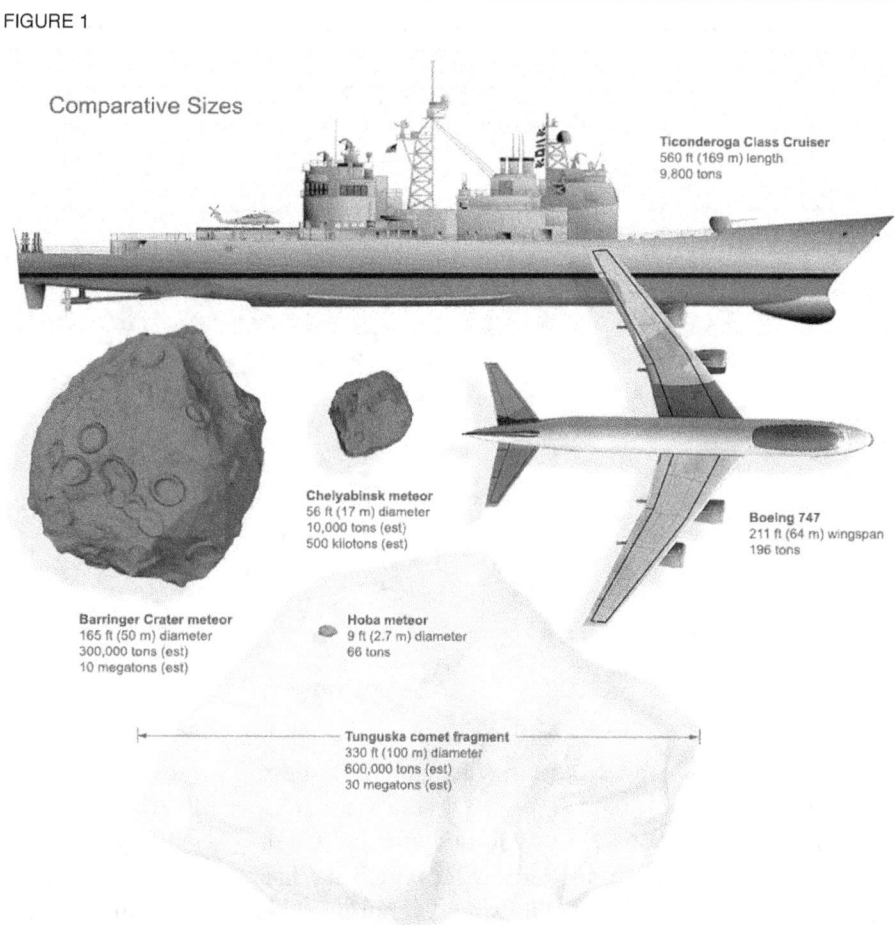

FIGURE 1

Comparative Sizes

Ticonderoga Class Cruiser
560 ft (169 m) length
9,800 tons

Chelyabinsk meteor
56 ft (17 m) diameter
10,000 tons (est)
500 kilotons (est)

Boeing 747
211 ft (64 m) wingspan
196 tons

Barringer Crater meteor
165 ft (50 m) diameter
300,000 tons (est)
10 megatons (est)

Hoba meteor
9 ft (2.7 m) diameter
66 tons

Tunguska comet fragment
330 ft (100 m) diameter
600,000 tons (est)
30 megatons (est)

Image © TheObjectReport.com

both Bush and Obama. But this issue has come back up again. It was in 2012 that the Russians refloated the offer, and it was named the *Strategic Defense of Earth* in some of the news coverage. They said: Why don't we have a joint cooperative program for a Strategic Defense of Earth against the threats of asteroids and related issues? Now, today, with the prospect of a real shift in the United States, assuming we can contain Obama and he doesn't return to his murderous orientation as Mr. LaRouche has warned, we could actually see this principle emerge and become a central pillar of a new historical era today.

The Asteroid Threat

We thought it would be appropriate, today, to start to put this issue back on the table. I want to start by illustrating some of what these threats are, what we're facing in terms of the threats to the Earth from these objects in our Solar system. If we go to the slide-show, we have a first graphic [**Fig. 1**] illustrating the reality

FIGURE 2

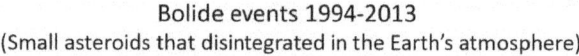

Bolide events 1994-2013
(Small asteroids that disintegrated in the Earth's atmosphere)

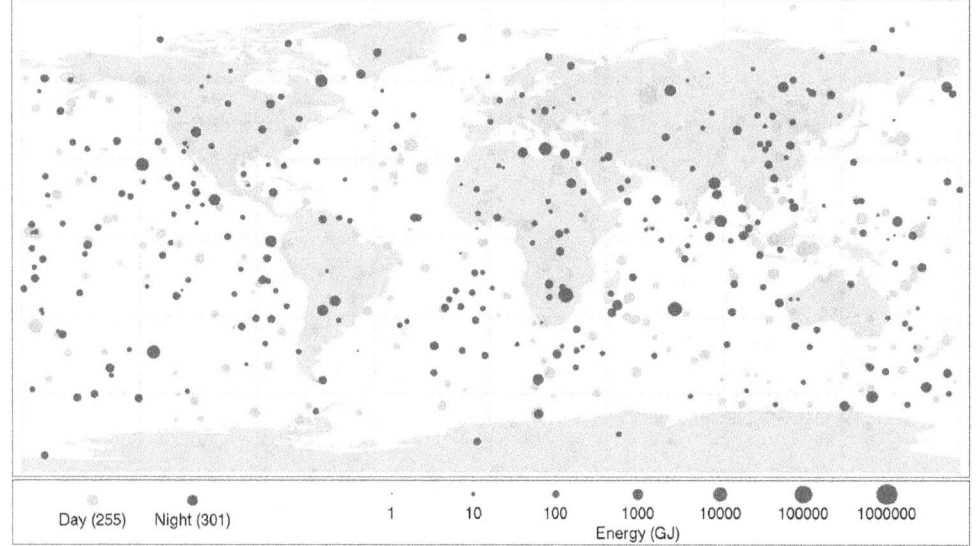

Day (255)   Night (301)

1   10   100   1000   10000   100000   1000000

Energy (GJ)

NASA

the largest in this time range; these others were smaller than the Chelyabinsk impact, but these were still large explosions in the upper atmosphere. You can see that they've painted the entire Earth over the course of this time period. These impacts are constantly occurring.

To give another sense of defending the Earth from these asteroids, here is a schematic of the inner Solar system [**Fig. 3**]. You can see Jupiter's orbit as the farthest orbit out there; then comes Mars, and Earth's orbit is a little bit darker than the other orbits. All of these blue lines—assuming you have high resolution to see the details of this visual—this blue haze you might see is actually composed of over 1,400 orbits of asteroids that are specifically classified as particularly hazardous asteroids. These are asteroids whose orbits cross the Earth's orbit at some point and create the potential, where the asteroid is at the intersection at the same time as the Earth, and you have an impact, a collision. You can see here how crowded the inner Solar system is.

Fortunately, among these that we know of, none of these is expected to hit in the next century or any foreseeable time-frame. This alone looks pretty dense, pretty packed in the inner Solar system here. What people should really get their mind around is that this is a tiny fraction of what we expect to be out there.

We can see here, if we take a little bit more complicated graphic [**Fig. 4**] and break it down, there are literally hundreds of thousands to millions of asteroids of the size of the Chelyabinsk meteor, or bigger, that we have not yet discovered. Based on our understanding of the distribution of asteroids of different sizes, we know that they are out there; we just don't know where they are. We don't know which ones might impact or which ones might not. We don't know when the impacts would be.

You can see in Figure 4 the relationship between

that these impacts happen, and they happen a lot more frequently than people tend to realize. In the animation, you can see the famous, very well-documented Chelyabinsk impact over Russia, an impact which we had no warning about; we did not know it was coming. This very small asteroid, which came in and impacted with a very high speed, which is characteristic of all of these collisions in the Solar system. A lot of the energy release is due to the fact that these speeds are incredibly fast.

When you get an impact of two orbiting bodies in the Solar system, you tend to get massive energy releases, explosions. Here you had a very small object intersecting the Earth, slamming into the atmosphere and releasing the energy of a small nuclear explosion as it hit. This awakened a lot of the world to the reality that these kinds of things do happen, and we have no defense.

One, we didn't even see this one coming; and two, if we had seen it coming, we have no demonstrated, developed capability to defend the Earth from these kinds of challenges. Additionally, I'd like to point people to some data that's been released in the relatively recent period, as we can see in this map of the world [**Fig. 2**], an illustration of many smaller meteor impacts into the atmosphere that have occurred just between 1994 and 2013. The Chelyabinsk impact was

FIGURE 3

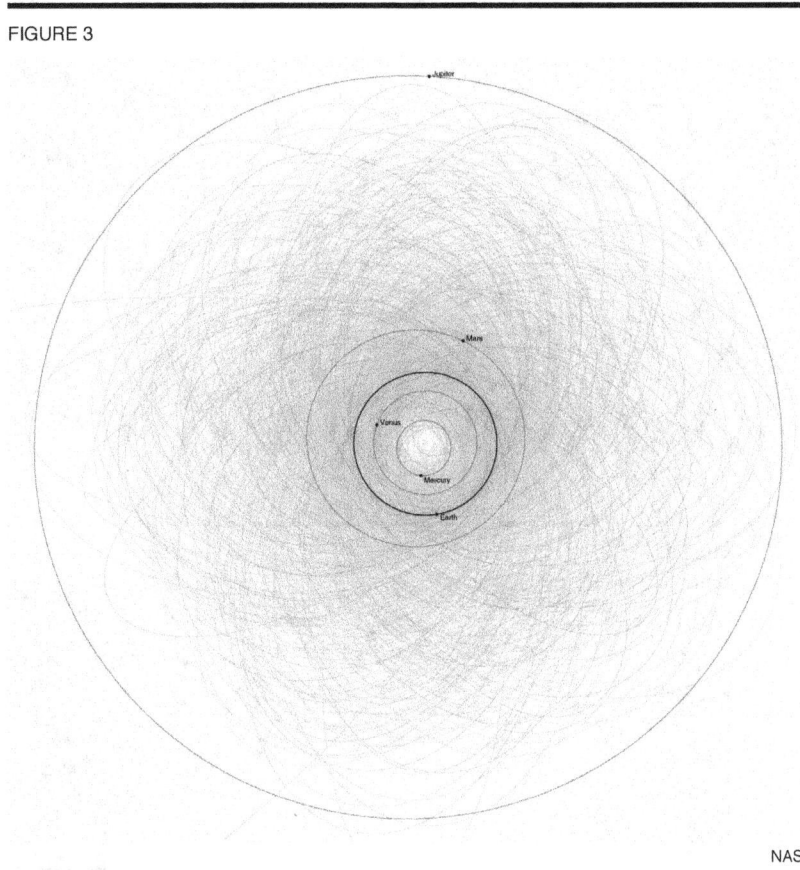

NASA

FIGURE 4

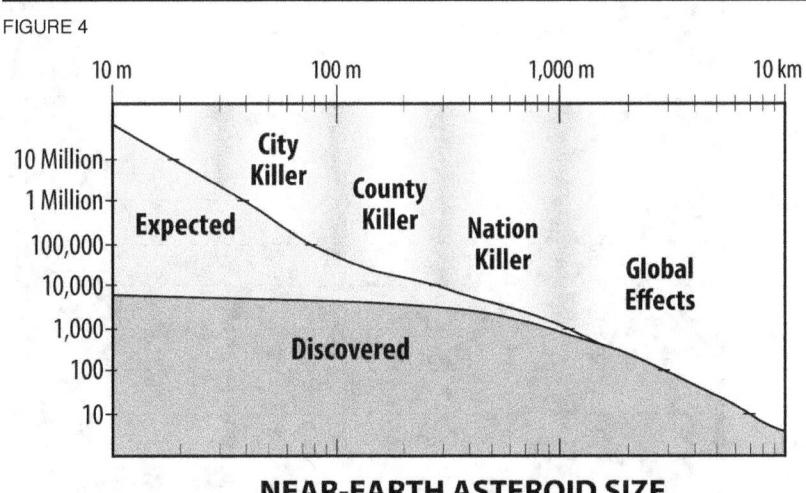

NEAR-EARTH ASTEROID SIZE

Ben Deniston

different sizes of near-Earth asteroids on the horizontal axis in a logarithmic scale. On the far right, you can see the very large ones in the range of kilometers in diameter, all the way down to sizes of meters. On the vertical axis, you can see the expected estimates of the distribution, the number, of near-Earth asteroids of those sizes.

You can see for the very large ones, we believe there are not very many; but as you start to get to smaller sizes, you get a geometric growth in the number of near-Earth asteroids of these different sizes.

You can also see the scale of the damage depicted, that would be inflicted on the Earth if one were to hit over an unlucky location. The Chelyabinsk impact was at the upper limit of one that doesn't do a huge amount of damage. But if it were just a little bigger, it could have caused really catastrophic effects for the entire region around Chelyabinsk, Russia. In this range, what people sometimes call a "city-killer" range, with an impact that would release the energy of a large thermonuclear explosion—we've discovered that about one percent of the near-Earth asteroids are in this size range.

Comets

NASA has done a good job of discovering a number of the larger objects which can do damage over a large fraction of the Earth—even potentially the entirety of the Earth. But as you start to go to these smaller sizes, we've barely scratched the surface. As dense as you think this previous graphic is in terms of the number of bodies out there, there are orders of magnitude more, that could do serious damage, that we just don't know about. Again, the first step is knowing where they are and when they might hit; the second step is actually having a defense capability. We've not really done anything besides general studies and theoretical investigations on that front. So, this is still an open, unanswered challenge.

All of this, however, is just the first step in a real defense of the planet Earth from these types of cosmic challenges. Additionally, as people are probably aware, there is also the issue of comets. This really grabbed people's attention in the mid '90s when mankind sat on the planet Earth, looked to Jupiter, and watched a massive comet that had broken apart into a series of fragments—as you can see [**Fig. 5**]—collide with Jupiter. In the animation, you see the explosion of one of these

FIGURE 5

NASA

fragments as it impacted Jupiter's surface. The other bright object is one of Jupiter's moons, but this is an image in the infrared where you can see the effects of these energetic types of activities more clearly. In the purple image [**Fig. 6**], you can clearly see the effects of the impact on the surface of Jupiter after the impact had occurred. These impacts left marks the size of the planet Earth on Jupiter's surface.

So, this was a big wake-up call in the mid '90s. This was comet Shoemaker-Levy 9. Before this period, it wasn't widely accepted that we had to think about these types of impacts. When this occurred, and they found this stream of comet fragments about a year before it actually hit, they looked at its orbit and said, "Wow! This is going hit Jupiter." So, everyone was sitting there watching as this thing went in. We had the Hubble telescope, all these telescopes pointing; we saw this thing as well as we could from all over the world. This really was a major wake-up call to the fact that these impacts really do occur. They can come from asteroids, which you saw in the illustration of the inner Solar system, but they can also come from comets. This represents a qualitatively different challenge, as we'll see in the next anima-tion.

This should give you a sense of this greater, more difficult, challenge posed by comets. This is a particular case of a comet named C1996B2, and this was discovered on Jan. 31, 1996. That's when we first knew this comet even existed. As you can see in the animation, which is based directly on the orbital data from NASA, we discovered this comet when it was just out

FIGURE 6

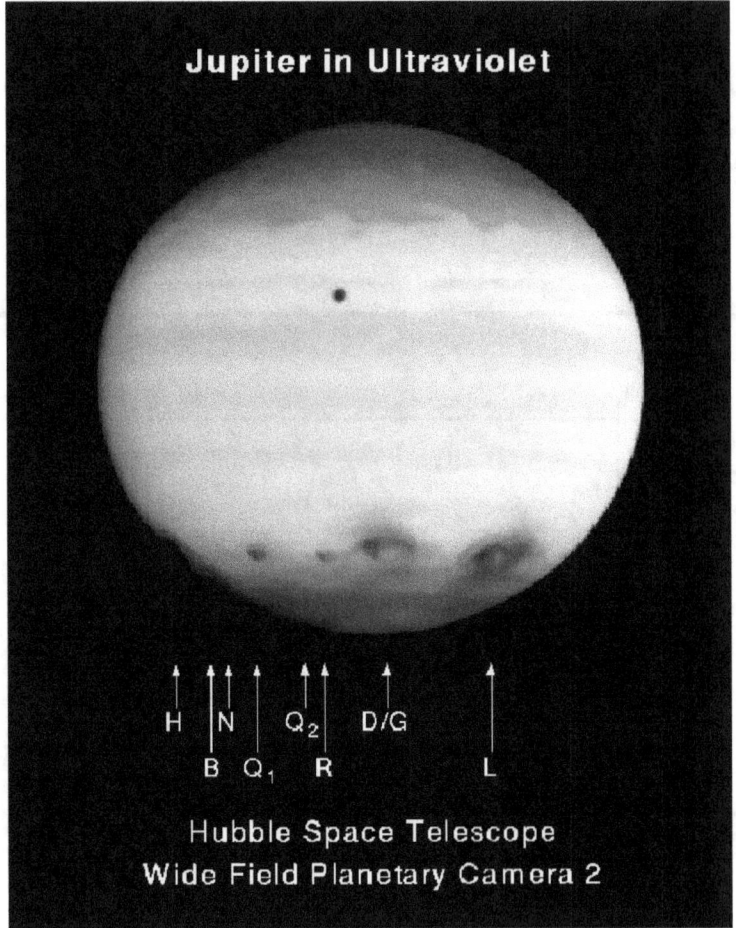

Jupiter in Ultraviolet

H N Q₂ D/G
B Q₁ R L

Hubble Space Telescope
Wide Field Planetary Camera 2

NASA

past the orbit of Mars. Within two months, it made a close pass by the Earth. We had no idea it was out there until *two months* before it made a close pass by the Earth. Whereas the object that hit over Russia—the Chely-

FIGURE 7

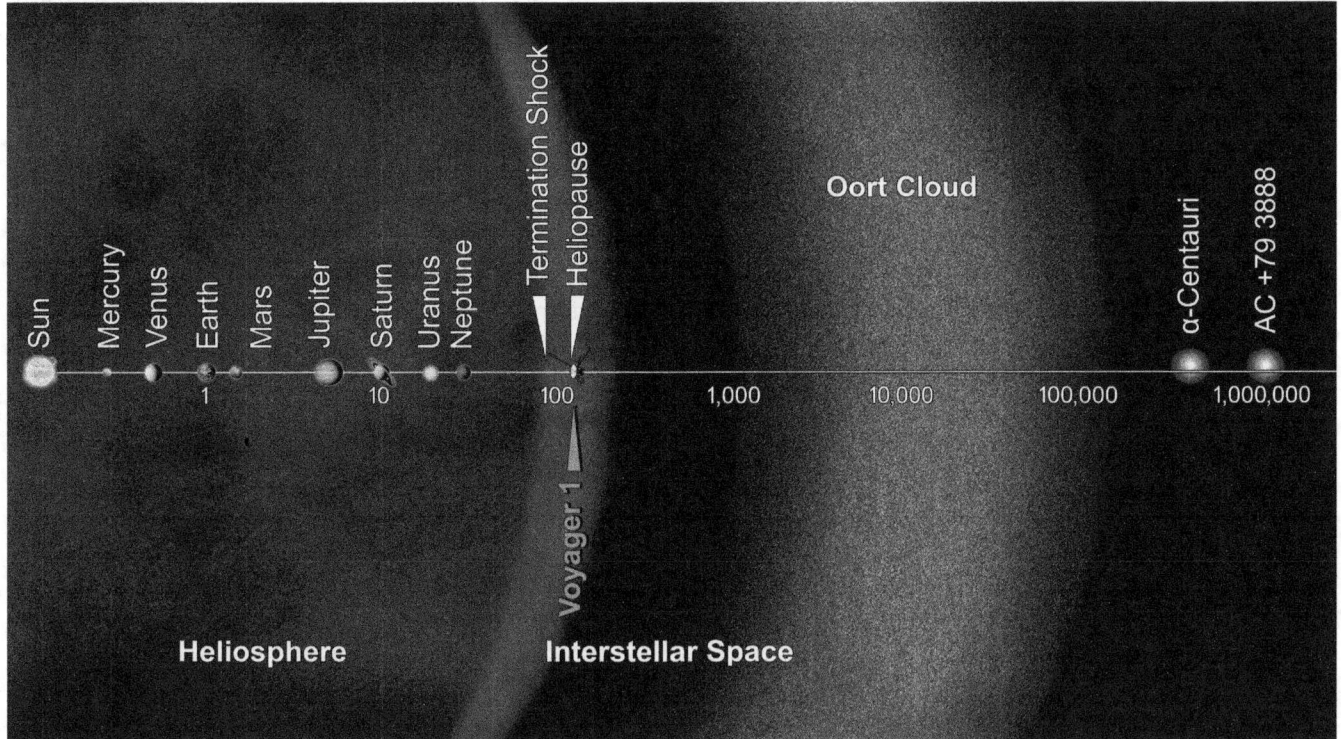

NASA

abinsk impact—was measured at about twenty meters in diameter, the comet C1996B2 is estimated to be about five *kilometers* in diameter. That's about half the diameter of the comet that's believed to have taken out the dinosaurs. As we let the animation play out, we see something very interesting that's characteristic of this distinct nature of the challenge of comets. Look at its orbit.

The circular orbits you see here are the outer planets, but comets have extremely elliptical orbits that take them far out into the depths of the Solar system. When these comets are out there in the far reaches of the Solar system, they're incredibly difficult to see. So, we only see them when they're starting to come into the inner Solar system. Again, as this case demonstrated, we saw this one only two months before it made a close pass. If that had been on an impact trajectory, there would have been nothing we could have done. A comet of that size is one which could wipe out civilization. We're not talking about the local-scale damage of the asteroids; we're talking about catastrophic effects across the whole planet.

Mastering the Entire Solar System

So, this is another depiction [**Fig. 7**] of where we think these bodies are. Based on the orbits of these

comets—sometimes technically referred to as long period comets—it's believed that many of these comets reside in the farthest reaches of the Solar system, far, far beyond the outer planets. This is a logarithmic scale, so you can see that this distribution of comets—sometimes referred to as the Oort Cloud—begins over tens of times past where Voyager has currently reached, and extends tens of times farther than that. We're talking about the very outskirts of the gravitational hold of the Sun. We haven't seen this region, but based on the orbits of comets that have been observed in just the short time period mankind has been able to make these observations, it is believed that there is a very large population of bodies out in this outer region of the Solar system. Because the gravitational effect of the Sun is so weak out there, it doesn't take much to perturb their orbits and potentially send some into the inner Solar system. Again, with our current capabilities, we only see them months, maybe if we're lucky a few years, before an impact, certainly not enough time to do anything about it with our current capabilities.

There are some studies—although the data is limited—indicating there might be a certain cyclical nature to these large comet impacts. Some people even believe it could relate to how the Solar system moves through the Galaxy, which raises some very interesting questions about how this outer region of comets could get perturbed on a periodic basis and send in what they call "showers"—i.e., cometary showers of many comets coming into the inner Solar system, creating a scenario where it's much more likely that Earth or the other planets might get hit with an impact, as Jupiter got hit in the '90s.

It's worth noting that one of the leading astronomers in this whole field, Eugene Shoemaker, who unfortunately passed away in the late '90s, had pioneered much of the work in this field. The comet that impacted Jupiter is named after him; he and his wife discovered it together. Shoemaker believed that it is likely that *we are currently in a period of a "comet shower."* He published articles on this in the late '90s. Based upon types of crater records and other evidence, he said it's not certain, but it could be the case, that we're currently in the middle of what on a human time scale is a long period in which there's an increased frequency of cometary entries into the inner Solar system and an increased likelihood of impacts occurring.

Relevant to this hypothesis, it was only last year that we found out that a relatively dim star had actually passed through the Oort Cloud about 70,000 years ago—this being one of the scenarios that can perturb many of these bodies. Again, since these things are so far away, it can take 70,000 years for the effects of such an occurrence to reach the inner Solar system. The point is, this is still incredibly preliminary knowledge of this region—of the Oort Cloud and of the region between the Oort Cloud and the inner Solar system. There could be a long-period comet that's only ten years out, that's been travelling for 50,000 years from the Oort Cloud, or even longer, and it's now only ten years away on a direct impact course with the Earth, and we wouldn't even know. It could be just in the outskirts of the outer planets region of the Solar system, not even in the far, far depths region. Again, we're talking about things that can devastate civilization completely, globally, as we know it.

This discovery of this dim star passing through the Oort Cloud 70,000 years ago, we just found that out a year ago. How many other bodies are out there that might have had close passes in the geologically recent past that could be creating similar effects? The point is, our knowledge is incredibly minuscule for something that threatens the entire planet, and our defense capability doesn't exist. This typifies one of the issues that is front and center for this principle of the SDI, the SDE, to re-emerge, and for nations to come together and cooperate to combat this threat. These are threats that don't recognize national borders; they don't recognize cultural boundaries. They challenge the entire planet, and they are outside of our current capabilities. If we are going to have a sane and principled relationship of the leading nations on our planet, then it has to return to these kinds of challenges. The task is to recognize these common aims and to address these threats, as Dr. Edward Teller had spoken of, as Mr. LaRouche put on the table with the whole SDI proposal.

Mankind's Future

The point we should really end on, and maybe discuss a little bit in conclusion, is that—and this is something that we've been discussing with Mr. LaRouche over the recent weeks—this isn't a separate, isolated issue. This is part of mankind becoming a Solar system species. This is part of mankind expanding to a new level, developing a platform of economic activity that makes mankind a presence, an active force in the Solar system. We can come up with specific scenarios, where you can deflect one asteroid, or maybe develop a new telescope that might help us see some of these things—and we should be discussing and looking at those things. But the fundamental issue is, how do we expand mankind into the Solar system as a much more active and capable presence, where we can handle these kinds of challenges? How do we engage other nations in cooperation and collaboration, instead of hiding our technology and hiding our capabilities because we want to have a leg up over China or Russia? How do we jointly develop the fundamental science and technologies mankind needs to defend the planet Earth in an open, cooperative way?

If we're going to seriously get into that, Mr. LaRouche has been emphatic: this takes us right to the work of Krafft Ehricke, to LaRouche's collaboration with Krafft Ehricke, and to those early space pioneers who really worked out the fundamental principles of mankind's development of the Solar system. I think that this must be fully integrated with this Strategic Defense of Earth perspective. This must become a critical part of this new space paradigm that we've been discussing in recent weeks.

Return to the Road of Infinite Progress: Revive a Crash Program for Fusion Power

by Megan Beets

This article is an introduction to a coming series of weekly articles by the LaRouche PAC Science Research Team regarding the critical role of fusion power, space exploration, and the creative powers of the human mind in shaping the coming establishment of the new international paradigm of relations among great civilizations.

Contrary to the un-natural environmentalist ideology which still underlies the thinking of most in the trans-Atlantic nations today, mankind *must always grow*—both in number, and in the power it exerts in and over nature. This is not a choice; it is our essential species characteristic, not shared by any animal, and it is one the universe depends on for its continuing improvement and development.

Today, the world population is approaching 7.5 billion, and is growing exponentially. Under the "greenie" system—one which sees man as an animal—any increase in resource consumption required to provide a high standard of living to each and every human individual is horrific, an unthinkable "looting" of the planet's limited riches—a policy which must be stopped at all costs!

This outlook is a scientific fraud, and is part of a dying empire system.

To a healthy civilization, as with the "New Paradigm" intention of China to eliminate poverty worldwide, each of these 7.5 billion persons is, in potential, an indispensable resource for the next creative breakthrough for humanity—a breakthrough which creates new resources and potentials.

When U.S. policy was centered on a commitment to progress for all mankind, such as under John F. Kennedy, rather than geopolitics, we had intensive crash-programs both in space travel/colonization, and in harnessing the incredible potentials of the atomic nucleus in the form of fusion power.

Before those programs were sabotaged and all but shut down, the participating scientists had the natural and optimistic view that humanity was on the verge of overcoming poverty, disease, and energy shortages for good, relegating these problems to a bygone era.

What did those scientists see in the potentials of fusion power and the space program, of which most people today are completely ignorant? What happened (and is happening) in the U.S. fusion program? How might we revive this today?

For that, we must look to the remaining potentials in the U.S., and to the leadership of China. But first, consider a controversial fact.

> **"Our children will enjoy in their homes electrical energy too cheap to meter... It is not too much to expect that our children will know of great periodic regional famines in the world only as matters of history, will travel effortlessly over the seas and under them and through the air with a minimum of danger and at great speeds, and will experience a lifespan far longer than ours, as disease yields and man comes to understand what causes him to age."**
>
> *—Lewis Strauss, Chairman of the Atomic Energy Commission, 1954*

Population Growth Is Natural, and Good

The truth about mankind, unlike all animals, is that we are willfully creative. This means that we have the capacity to change nature in an increasingly powerful way by applying new discoveries of scientific and cultural principles to our work and life. For this, we are "rewarded" with an increased potential for both population density and lifespan.

For example, the late 19th/early 20th Century introduction of electricity into processes of industry, transportation, and agriculture revolutionized the quality and quantity of the productive output per capita, far beyond anything possible before. In this respect, man's power to change the planet—to create new materials and states of matter, higher energy throughput in plants and animals, large-scale construction of infra-

Max Planck Institute

The Wendelstein 7-X experimental stellarator reactor in Greifswald, Germany.

structure—has increased in an exponential way since our very beginning.

The growth in our species' power does not come about gradually; rather, each introduction of a discovery of a hitherto unknown principle (e.g. electromagnetism) has resulted in great, revolutionary leaps upward in our productive powers of labor per capita—and most importantly in our minds' increased powers to make the next scientific breakthrough. Therefore, it is in the interest of all mankind that each person—a potential source of the next discovery—enjoys a stable standard of living, and has access to the highest educational and cultural resources possible.

The challenges this poses for an ever-growing and longer-living population can only be overcome if we organize our society around the mission of discovering ever-higher principles of nature, expanding our dominion over this planet, and colonizing other bodies in our Solar system. For this, we must make the leap to fusion power.

The Optimism of Nuclear Fusion

Nuclear fusion is the joining together of two atomic nuclei—the process which powers the Sun—and it is no easy task to replicate this stellar phenomenon in the conditions on the surface of the Earth. It requires (under one hypothesis) the creation and handling/control of hot gases—plasmas—at temperatures many times hotter than the center of the Sun, which continue to behave in ways that defy our assumptions about the of nature of matter.

But what is so promising about achieving controlled fusion? In quantitative terms, the power density in an atomic nucleus is upwards of a billion times greater than that of the chemical forces contained in molecules. In terms of fuels, each gram of nuclear fusion fuel (deuterium-tritium) is 1,000 times more energy-dense than nuclear fission fuel (uranium-235), and up to one million times more energy dense than chemical fuels (hydrogen-oxygen combustion).

In order to obtain fuel for fusion, we will mine the oceans for the plentiful heavy hydrogen (deuterium) contained in seawater, and later, mine the Moon for the optimal fusion fuel held in the lunar soil, helium-3.

In qualitative terms, with full control over the atomic nucleus—both fission and fusion—humanity establishes a completely new relationship to materials and energies. We will, for example, be able to create new, specialty steels and other metals on a mass scale; manufacture medical isotopes when and wherever needed; mine our landfills for resources with the fusion torch; power a scientific colony and industrial operations on the Moon during the long lunar nights; and power a fusion-driven rocket for a trip of weeks, rather than months, to Mars and planets beyond, extending our reach into the Solar system.

Incredible progress has been made toward the mastery of fusion in the U.S. and internationally, beginning in the 1950s. If the trajectory established in the early decades of the U.S. fusion program had continued, then mastery of fusion as a power source would already be providing nations of the world with virtually unlimited energy, and would have created a qualitative transformation in our powers of industry, transportation, and medicine.

While the U.S. budget for fusion has been cut year after year—thus crippling a successful and necessary endeavor—China has today become the only nation in the world which is increasing its fusion budget, and has the intention to graduate 2,000 new fusion scientists by 2020.

In Part II, we will take up the current state of the U.S. fusion program (and its promising recent achievements), as well as the important developments of the past 15 months in Europe and Asia.

Every Day Counts In Today's Showdown To Save Civilization

That's why you need EIR's **Daily Alert Service**, a strategic overview compiled with the input of Lyndon LaRouche, and delivered to your email 5 days a week.

The election of Donald Trump to the Presidency of the Untied States has launched a new global era whose character has yet to be determined. The Obama-Clinton drive toward confrontation with Russia has been disrupted--but what will come next?

Over the next weeks and months there will be a pitched battle to determine the course of the Trump Administration. Will it pursue policies of cooperation with Russia and China in the New Silk Road, as the President-Elect has given some signs of? Will it follow through against Wall Street with Glass-Steagall?

The opposition to these policies will be fierce. If there is to be a positive outcome to this battle, an informed citizenry must do its part--intervening, educating, inspiring. That's why you need the EIR Daily Alert more than ever.

TUESDAY, NOVEMBER 22, 2016

Volume 3, Number 65

EIR Daily Alert Service

P.O. Box 17390, WASHINGTON, DC 20041-0390

- Only Global Solutions, Based on New Principles, Can Work
- Tulsi Gabbard Meets with Donald Trump Regarding Syria
- Robert Kagan Throws in the Towel, Complains U.S. Is Becoming 'Solipsistic'
- War Party Moving To Preempt Trump-Putin Reset
- Syrian Army Makes More Progress in Aleppo
- Duterte Gives OK to Nuclear Power for Philippines
- Europe Will Suffer from Maintaining Russia Sanctions
- Former Chilean Diplomat Confirmed, 'We Will Joyfully Welcome Xi Jinping'
- Duterte and Putin Establish Philippines-Russia Cooperation
- François Fillon, Pro-Russian Thatcherite, Wins First Round of French Right-Wing Presidential Primary

EDITORIAL

Only Global Solutions, Based on New Principles, Can Work

III. The End of War?

PROJECT PHOENIX

Aleppo Will Rise From the Ashes of War

by Hussein Askary and Ulf Sandmark

Dec. 19—Two days ago, the Syrian city of Aleppo was finally liberated from the barbaric forces of Obama's Anglo-Saudi takfiri terrorists. After almost five years of their occupation of the eastern part of the city and the north of the province, this second largest city in Syria—a thriving economic and cultural center of the nation—has been reduced to little more than a heap of rubble.

In the 2004 census, the population of the whole Province of Aleppo was 4.4 million, half of which, 2.1 million, lived in the city of Aleppo. The private sector dominated the city's economy, reflecting the population's high degree of entrepreneurship, with the majority working in small and medium industries and commerce. Sixty percent of the workforce was employed in productive enterprises, of which 25 percent was in manufacturing. Aleppo was the manufacturing power-house of Syria, as it was home to 30-40 percent of national manufacturing. The City's export share was around 35 percent of Syria's total non-oil exports. Moreover, Aleppo dominated both textiles and pharmaceutical industries in the country. The city had a substantial presence in all four subsectors of manufacturing: the textiles, chemical, engineering, and food-processing sectors.

Modern Industrial Ambitions

The Sheikh Najjar industrial city is located 10 km north east of Aleppo's city boundaries. Its construction was begun in the year 2000. This city, with its area of 4,412 hectares, included industry, housing, infrastructure, green areas, commercial services, and administrative areas. In 2009, 413 industrial firms were already operating there, and an additional 1,129 were under construction. Its industrial area, which had been provided with world standard-infrastructure, was divided into three zones: light industry, medium-sized, and heavy industry.

Fighting inside the industrial city between the rebels and government forces has now turned the Sheikh

www.hollilla.com

The Arch entrance into western Sheikh Najjar Industrial City.

Damaged building in Sheikh Najjar Industrial City, near Aleppo, Syria.

Najjar industrial city into little more than a ghost town. The Sheikh Najjar Industrial City was a very good example of the intentions of the Syrian government to pursue a process of industrialization. This process must be revived under the reconstruction process.

Project Phoenix

Aleppo is the oldest continuously inhabited city in the world. It has existed for more than 10,000 years. Since ancient times, Aleppo has been a hub of world trade between East and West, and its perfect position between the Mediterranean and Mesopotamia made it a major trade center. Throughout its long history, Aleppo has witnessed many moments of greatness and decline, survived massive turmoil and earthquakes both physical and social, and yet each time arose again like the Phoenix bird. The people and government of Syria have kept that same spirit alive today, in the face of the worst crisis in the country's history.

In November 2015, a delegation of the Schiller Institute and the Syrian-Swedish Committee for Democracy (including the co-author of this article, Ulf Sandmark) travelled to Damascus to bring humanitarian aid to the war-torn country, but more importantly, to present to the highest levels of the Syrian government, the Schiller Institute's "Project Phoenix" for the reconstruction of Syria.

Project Phoenix consisted of three major sections:

1. How to mobilize the physical, intellectual and moral potential of the nation for reconstruction;

2. How to finance reconstruction; and

3. How Syria can benefit from connecting to the New Silk Road.

Certain developments in the past two years speak to the Schiller Institute's intervention and prove it to be timely and correct. The intervention of the BRICS nations in 2014 to change the decaying and destructive world order, was a major incentive for the Syrian people to follow this new paradigm. Thereafter, the direct military intervention by Russia in September 2015 in support of the Syria army and people in fighting the terrorists and forces of the dark ages, has set the stage for a completely new political and strategic geometry in that country and the whole region.

On top of the Russian military intervention, on the economic side, Chinese President Xi Jinping brought the concept of the New Silk Road to southwest Asia and the Arab world in January 2016, during his visit to Egypt, Saudi Arabia, and Iran. Chinese and Russian government officials have visited Syria and offered to help in the reconstruction process. The Syrian Investment Agency (SIA) announced in April 2016 that it intended to organize a reconstruction conference together with the BRICS nations in the near future.

In the mean time, in February 2016, *Executive Intelligence Review* produced an Arabic version of its special report *The New Silk Road Becomes the World Land-Bridge,* with an added feature on Project Phoenix. In this Arabic version, Helga Zepp-LaRouche, Chairwoman of the Schiller Institute, argued that connecting the Middle East to the New Silk Road project would be a key element for establishing peace and development in this region.

Financing Reconstruction in a Ruined Nation

A Hamiltonian national credit system can kick off the reconstruction process, despite the fact that most of a country's previous physical economy and financial capacities are devastated. Examples like the newly founded United States in the late 18th Century, or Germany after World War II, can serve to demonstrate how a nation can mobilize to rebuild itself after a destructive war.

Manufacturing plant in Sheikh Najjar Industrial City.

The starting point for a credit system is a vision of reconstruction. This should include a centralized development plan, declaring step by step what the nation intends to accomplish at defined future dates. With this plan as the foundation, the government can issue the necessary credit to put the available workforce, tools, and materials to work. The projects can be run by either private entrepreneurs or government authorities.

For issuing this reconstruction credit, the government needs an institution devoted to rebuilding the nation, such as a National Bank or a special "Reconstruction Bank," with majority Syrian state control over its stocks and policies. Special "Hamiltonian credit" should be provided by the state, either directly (through the Treasury) or through the central bank, to the Reconstruction Bank. It can also raise additional domestic capital for this bank in a way similar to Egypt's mobilization of its people to finance the expanded Suez Canal: by stock offerings directly to the citizens of Syria at home or in the diaspora. With such a credit mechanism, the government can create enough credit for the rapid reconstruction of Syria.

Furthermore, credits from private banks should be strictly controlled, to ensure that they are directed in accordance with the reconstruction plan, as categories of loans necessary for the physical needs of industries and the people. The expansion of credit is thus tied to the real economy.

A domestic Hamiltonian credit system can enable national labor and resources to be fully employed and utilized, but it cannot pay for what needs to be imported. Usually, for that purpose, foreign currency, primarily from export income, is used. But that alone will not suffice for the massive reconstruction and development efforts needed. Syria will need huge loans in foreign currency, to be able to import needed machines and equipment. These loans may be linked to the reconstruction plan and the value of the projects being financed. They can also be part of export-credit agreements with industrialized nations to help import the needed machinery and technology into the country. In this way, the loans and their interest rates can be adapted to the long-term repayment possibilities derived from the projects they support.

The BRICS New Development Bank and the Asian Infrastructure Investment Bank (AIIB) have been established to provide credit based on the potential of each project into the future, rather than being based only on the current payment capacity of the nation initiating the project. Thus, Syria has great potential to obtain financing in foreign currency for important large-scale infrastructure projects.

Textile plant in Sheikh Najjar Industrial City.

Physical-Economic Development

Reconstruction can be oriented to creating an infrastructure platform with the highest possible level of technology and productivity. A major upgrade of the chemical industry, based on oil and gas resources, can promote new industries producing fertilizers, plastics, pharmaceuticals, and other high-tech products. In line with the BRICS paradigm, the nuclear industry that was destroyed by Israel and by sanctions, can be resurrected both for power production and water desalination.

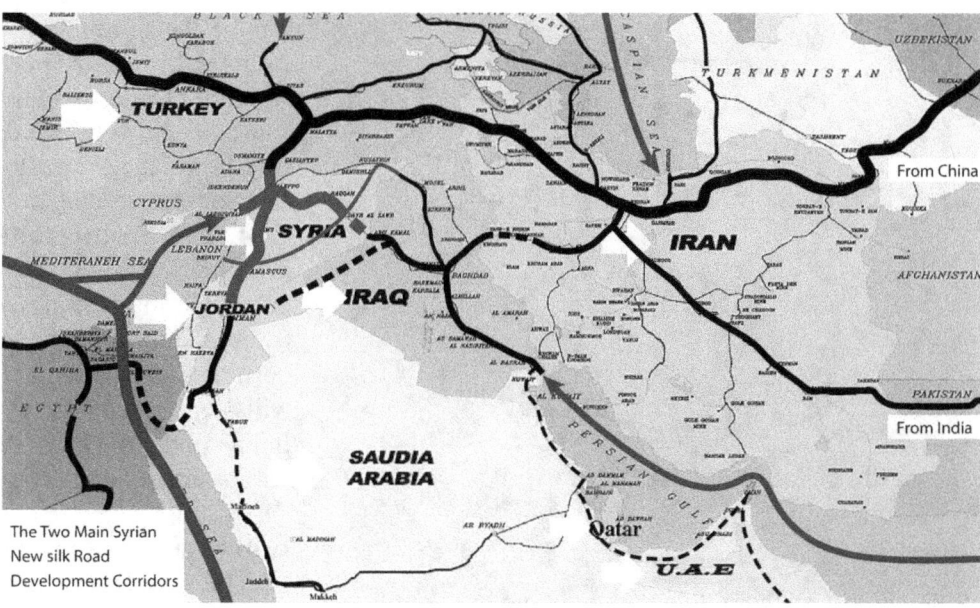

The Two Main Syrian New silk Road Development Corridors

The targeting and destruction of the Syrian pharmaceuticals industry by the enemy underscores its strategic importance, and the same goes for the embattled oil, gas, and petrochemical sectors. Also, the processing of cotton and other agricultural products in Syria's renowned textile industry is a major reconstruction task, in addition to building other industries. Temporary work brigades mobilizing the unemployed could be financed in the same way, to build what is needed, while training the unemployed for higher-skill work. The Army Corps of Engineers could provide the kernel of these work brigades, and with such reconstruction projects continue its defense of the Syrian people.

Syria's national transport routes have to adapt to transcontinental routes from the Mediterranean Sea, the Indian Ocean, the Red Sea, the Caspian Sea, and the Black Sea. This was the vision of President Bashar Assad in his "Five Seas Strategy," which he pronounced in 2009 before this war was waged on Syria.

The New Silk Road strategy involves not only transportation alone, but international development corridors, which will bring long-term vitality and growth to the ancient crossroads of Syria. Besides railways, they include pipelines, water projects, industrial zones, agriculture, and city-building.

Syria and the New Silk Road

Syria enjoys a perfect position between three continents, Asia, Europe, and Africa, and also between major bodies of water. Thus, it can connect to both the Eurasian-African Land-Bridge and Economic Belt of the New Silk Road, and to the Maritime Silk Road.

1. The West/East land route to Baghdad, Tehran and Asia. The New Silk Road Economic Belt extends from China to Central Asia and Iran, and further to Turkey and Europe. The Iranian transportation plans extend eastward to Iraq, Baghdad, and further along both Tigris and Euphrates rivers to Syria. The branch on the Euphrates River can also be connected to the Maritime Silk Road through the Persian Gulf and the port of Basra in southern Iraq, and northwest towards Deir Ezzour, Raqqa, and Aleppo. The old Silk Road along the Euphrates River from Basra on the Persian Gulf will reach into Syria, and from there, a railway connection to Europe through Turkey. Such a Euphrates railway, built in cooperation with Iraq, will be a big step toward regional integration and a development corridor extending from Persian Gulf, the Arabian Sea, and the Indian Ocean to the Eastern Mediterranean and Southern Europe.

Another step to open up the old East-West Silk Road routes will be to build a 200-km railway from Deir Ezzor southwest to Palmyra, the legendary Silk Road city. This missing link will allow railway service from Tehran and Baghdad through these Syrian cities and onward, in the same direction, to Damascus and Beirut on the Mediterranean.

2. The north-south link to Egypt and Africa. A more direct land transport corridor can link Syria to

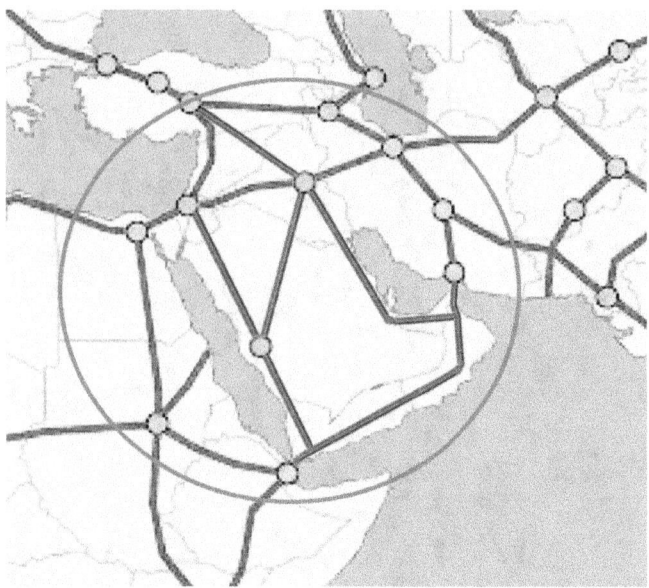

Syria is the link between Asia, Europe, and Africa.

the dynamically developing economy of Egypt through rebuilding the historical north-south transportation route in western Syria, also known as the Hijaz Railway from Turkey that runs south from Aleppo to Damascus, continuing to Amman, Jordan. Syria's relationship with Egypt's planned giant industrial zones along the New Suez Canal will be boosted by the railway link from Cairo to the Gulf of Aqaba, across the norther part of the Sinai Peninsula, and on to Amman. Moreover, Egypt and Saudi Arabia agreed in April 2016 to build a bridge across the Tiran Strait to the southern part of the Sinai Peninsula and northward across the Suez Canal Zone to Cairo. Syria and the Eastern Mediterranean and Asia will be connected to Africa through this transcontinental land-bridge across the Red Sea.

Lyndon LaRouche's "Oasis Plan for the Middle East," first publicized in *EIR* during the 1970s and revived in 1990 as the First Gulf War loomed, envisaged a north-south development corridor from Turkey to Egypt and Africa, running through Damascus, Syria's Golan Heights, into Israel and the Palestinian territories in the West Bank and Gaza, then to Sinai in Egypt. This was the dorrect basis for a durable Israeli-Palestinian peace process, which is currently almost completely dead.

3. The northern link from Europe, the Black Sea region, and Russia. The Black Sea region will be connected to Syria through Istanbul and another Turkish port, Samsun on the southern Black Sea coast. Istanbul is also the destination for the new Viking Rail Line from the Lithuanian port of Klaipeda on the Baltic Sea, which will be a trade route from the Baltic Sea region and Sweden, southward to Syria. This is the way that Russia and the Caucasus will also come closer to Syria and Southwest Asia.

4. The Mediterranean maritime link. Since the inauguration of Egypt's New Suez Canal in August 2015, enormous ships can now bring cargo flows from China and India on the Maritime Silk Road, to the Mediterranean Sea. Freight shipments and travel to Syria will then be possible via this canal and the Greek and Italian ports, if Syria's own Mediterranean Sea ports of Tartus and Latakia are expanded.

Conclusion

The population centers of Syria have historically evolved around the river systems and trade routes. Syria's seventeen million population are concentrated in the western part of the country, in cities lined along the north-south trade corridors from Aleppo, Homs, Hama, and Damascus. Another concentration is on the Mediterranean coast and the richly rain-fed agricultural regions of Latakia, Idlib, and western Aleppo. The other population concentration is in the east of the country, in the Jazirah region between the Euphrates and Tigris rivers. These are rich irrigated agricultural regions that also enjoy a great concentration of oil and gas resources, and hydropower.

From what is stated above, we can conclude that Syria enjoys all the necessary requisites for reconstruction: human and natural resources, strategic position, and a deep cultural heritage. In a peaceful and development-friendly international environment, Syria can quickly emerge out of the ashes of war.

As Helga Zepp-LaRouche, the Chairwoman of the Schiller Institute, stated on Dec. 17: "The tragedy of war is that in its course, horrors occur, especially when it rages on for many years and is in fact a proxy war instigated from the outside—and those horrors produce a never-ending chain of horrors. Therefore, it is all the more urgent now, that all neighbors of the region: Russia, China, India, Iran, Egypt, but also Germany, France and Italy, put large-scale reconstruction of the entire Middle East on the agenda."

The Liberation of Aleppo should be regarded as a turning point, not only in the history of Syria, but of that region and the world, in the direction of leading the world towards peace and development.

Sen. Gravel: 'Hacking the Election' Charge Is Ridiculous

Jason Ross of LaRouche PAC interviewed Mike Gravel, a Democratic U.S. Senator from Alaska 1968-81, on Dec. 14, and replayed and reported on the interview on LaRouche PAC's Weekly Webcast of Dec. 16. Edited excerpts follow.

Jason Ross: On Dec. 12, the VIPS group—the Veteran Intelligence Professionals for Sanity—released a memo called "Allegations of Hacking the Election Are Baseless," in which they gave their reasons for coming to that assessment. We interviewed a leading member of the VIPS group, Senator Mike Gravel—former Senator from Alaska— to get his take on this; and we can play that for you now.

LPAC

Senator Mike Gravel

Mike Gravel is one of the signers of a letter that was released by the Veteran Intelligence Professionals for Sanity a couple of days ago in response to the *New York Times* and the general media tumult around Russia hacking the elections—Russia denying Hillary Clinton the Presidency that she deserved as a gift from God. So, I'd like to ask Senator Gravel, who is a former adjutant top-secret control officer for the Communications Intelligence Service, and a special agent of the Counterintelligence Corps, in addition being a former Senator from Alaska. Senator Gravel, could you tell our viewers what you think of this notion that Russia hacked the election and determined the outcome of our Presidential election here in the U.S.?

Sen. Mike Gravel: First off, it's ridiculous! It's far-fetched ridiculous! We know—and here we can be grateful to Edward Snowden—that the United States' capability, along with their partners in Britain, have the capability of vacuuming up *every single communication in the world*. That means that the NSA has *all* of Hillary's emails; has *all* of the communications between the

U.S. and Russia. And so for the government to come out and say via the intelligence community, that this is all instigated by Russia, is just part of the demonization that we've seen taking place about Putin and Russia, as part of a plan in the United States to have regime change in Russia. Believe it. We're seeing what's happened in Syria with regime change, which is hundreds of thousands of people displaced and killed. And now we know that it was the U.S. that financed the coup in Kiev, that unseated Ukraine's duly-elected President, who was favorable to Russia; which, of course, is normal, since they are neighbors and were essentially one country at one point. And so we destabilized that, and that was admitted to by [the Assistant Secretary] Victoria Nuland, who's still there; was there under Clinton. She admitted that the United States had spent $5 billion over a 10-year period, to destabilize the government of Ukraine. We succeeded.

Then, of course, as a reaction to that, when Russia had to continue its fresh-water port, which is Sevastopol, which came under threat, they protected it by annexing it—*re*-annexing it, let's put it that way—because it was part of Russia before. It was given away by Nikita Khruschev several years ago.

So, in point of fact, we have all the knowledge in the NSA. Maybe the NSA doesn't talk to the FBI, or doesn't talk to the CIA. I don't know. We've had this problem in 9/11, with nobody connecting the dots; and may have that same problem right now. But there's no question that the United States government does more activity in the cyber world than *anybody else*. Russia is probably a distant second. China is a distant second. But there's nobody that holds a candle to what we're capable of doing.

So, for our government to turn around—or *elements*

youtube

*Director of National
Intelligence James Clapper*

CC/Mariusz Kubik

*Victoria Nuland, Assistant
Secretary of State*

Hillary Clinton

creative commons/Gage Skidmore

John Bolton

within our government, let's put it that way—to turn around and say that the Democratic Party was hacked and these hacks were given to WikiLeaks who then released them; well, it seems odd that the American government would have to be partners of WikiLeaks to let this stuff out. What seems more likely, is that somebody within the government, whether rogue or by intent, saw this as an ability to try and embarrass Russia; embarrass Putin, and to save face for Hillary, who was promptly losing the election with her skullduggery.

As a result of this, we now see the *New York Times*—and this should not surprise us—the *New York Times* and the *Washington Post*, the two major national newspapers of note, have done a lot of disinformation over the years, and I think this is just one more instance of that disinformation coming out of the *New York Times*. Keep in mind it's the *New York Times* that ginned up the war to invade Iraq. You can take your credits from there, as to what they're capable of doing when they put their mind to it.

So, that's essentially what I think is the case. Here too, we have enough people with skills and knowledge, particularly with our group, the former intelligence officers in the government, very senior intelligence officers—because none of us are spring chickens—to be able to question what has been put out, and say that this doesn't seem accurate, and doesn't make sense.

To Sabotage New Relations with Russia

Ross: All of this might look like it's a bunch of flailing around to explain the electoral defeat by blaming anybody except for the terrible candidate that the Democrats had, but it's much more than this. You have to remember, this isn't just domestic theatrics; the case is being made for—as Obama put it—a revenge attack or some kind of answer being made to Russia in some way or another. That is, threatening a nuclear-armed nation over allegations that have not been backed up with any specific evidence, and frankly, accusing Russia of things that the U.S. admits to doing all the time. So, we asked Senator Gravel, what was the intent; why the anti-Russian hysteria? Is this just about the election? What's the push for this? This is what he had to say:

Sen. Gravel: The intent is to sabotage the potential new relationship [with Russia]. That's what the intent is. But here too, I think Trump has his own areas of expertise in this regard. And the new Secretary of State designate, Rex Tillerson, he also has a great deal of experience with the Russian leadership. And so, as a result of that, they're going to dictate their own policy.

What we see right now, is the last regurgitation of a failed policy, one that was very dangerous. In demonizing Putin the way we've done in American media, Western media, and then turning around and levelling the charge at them that they are trying to destabilize Western and Eastern Europe—it's ridiculous. I know of no instance—and I would question anybody to quote an instance — where Russia has threatened anybody in the last decade in Eastern Europe and Europe proper. He sells them oil and gas; why would he want to destabilize his customers? It makes no sense at all. But to the neocons, who are intent on trying to protect the hegemonic position of the United States in the world, *this makes a lot of good sense for them.* They need to demonize Russia and Putin, they need to demonize Chinese President Xi Jinping and China, and assert our military prowess in the world. We have a significant economic position in the world, and these militarists feel they've got to shore that position up, with militaristic policies that make no sense at all.

What they should be doing, is joining with China in the New Silk Road ("One Belt, One Road"), to raise the economic level of the world to a higher level, and that would be the biggest contribution we could make to the well-being of people around the world, and to the issue of having world peace. That's what we should be doing. But that's not what's happening. What's happening is what we learned from the study of the "Thucydides Trap" [invoked by Harvard scholar Graham Allison], where the power which is the global power—which is the United States—is now facing the problem of an ascending power like China moving in and surpassing us. Well, our egos may not be able to take that, but certainly the people of the world could take it; because it would mean greater economic activity, on the part of China.

So, it's all mixed up with this insanity that exists within the American government, by a group of people called neocons. They start with Cheney. They go from Cheney/Rumsfeld, that crowd, into the present group of neocons. Here you have a person like John Bolton, who's being considered for the Number Two man at the State Department. I can't think of a person who's more idiotic, as a neocon, than John Bolton. I think Trump is just wantonly picking people, hither and yon, to satisfy the conservatives.

I think what they're going to find, is when these neo-conservatives attempt to assert policy positions that are at variance from Donald Trump, they're going to find they're short-lived. He'll fire them. He's done that on TV and he's used to that. "Give me the wrong advice, you're fired!" That's what you're going to see from a President who's going to be tweeting. He's going to be tweeting his policies to the American people and the world, all by himself, in his room, with his little computer.

Ross: You know, if you have time for one more question, I'd like to ask you about China, which you brought up. One of Trump's recent appointments was the former governor of Iowa, which is a state that President Xi Jinping of China has close ties to—having lived there for years, studying agriculture when he was a lower-level figure in the government. You brought up the "One Belt, One Road" as a potential for the U.S. to be involved in. It's currently something that, under the Obama administration, the U.S. has been opposing. The U.S. did not join the Asian Infrastructure Investment Bank; the U.S. urged other nations not to join it as well. What would you see as the proper or the best—what should the U.S. role in the world be? What should U.S. relations with China in particular be with regard to this program?

Sen. Gravel: Well, the U.S. role should, first and foremost, rest upon economic activity—raising the quality of life for the people in the United States and for the people in the world. That's the goal that China has set with respect to its "One Belt, One Road."

We oppose that because we are refusing to accept the fact that China is the ascendant power, and that within a couple decades, will be the Number One economic power in the world; but not the military power. If you just look at the amount of money they're spending, they spend about 10% of what we do on our defense posture. That demonstrates that they have no interest in becoming the militarily predominant power in the world. They're ceding that to the United States.

But that, of course, is not all that attractive, as you saw in Obama's "Pivot to Asia." Thank God that we have a new President, Duterte, in the Philippines, who is now creating a rapprochement to China, which is the most enlightened thing they could do. Their future is not with the United States; their future is as a player in the economy of Asia. That's what a rapprochement with China portends—that the Philippines will be the recipient of extensive "One Belt, One Road" financing to raise the standard of living in the Philippines, which used to be superior to many of the other countries in Asia, and is now in the lower brackets.

My recommendation for the United States and the new administration would be Trump negotiating his "deal." And the deal he can negotiate is that, yes, the United States will join with China, and will raise the economic threshold of the world.

Ross: That sounds like an excellent direction for the U.S. Do you have any other, final thoughts you'd like to leave for our viewers?

Sen. Gravel: No, not at all, except to thank the LaRouche organization for doing good work in advancing the cause of peace, and in advancing the cause of economic growth. The only way we are going to bring about world peace is when we raise the standard of living of the people throughout the world. Again, thank you for the good work in that regard.

Ross: Senator Mike Gravel, thank you very much.

AFTER THE LIBERATION OF ALEPPO

Germany Must Shape the G-20 Agenda with a Marshall Plan

by Helga Zepp-LaRouche, chairwoman of the German political party Civil Rights Movement Solidarity (BüSo)

Dec. 17—President Obama, in the last press conference of his term in office, accused Russia and Russian President Putin personally of having manipulated the American presidential election through cyber-attacks, and announced that there would be reprisals—some explicit and open, and others so that Russia would recognize the author. This announcement of covert operations should cause alarm worldwide—what kind of operation does he mean? Drone strikes, "collateral damage" of all sorts? Obama apparently wants to use his remaining time in the White House for a confrontation with Russia, a confrontation whose end is signaled by Trump's cabinet appointments. Clearly the neocons—in whose camp Obama belongs, given his continuation of the policies of Bush and Cheney—do not accept their loss of power.

This is all the more outrageous as numerous representatives of the American intelligence community, as well as cyber-experts, have vehemently countered the allegation of President Obama and CIA Director John Brennan, that Putin personally oversaw cyber-attacks that led to the election of Trump. In a memorandum released December 12, the Veteran Intelligence Professionals for Sanity (VIPS)—among whom are former U.S. Senator Mike Gravel and former CIA agent Ray McGovern—stressed that these allegations have "no basis in fact." They state they have gone through the various claims about hacking and could say unambiguously, on the basis of their experience as experts in cyber-security, that what happened involved "leaks"—that is, the disclosure of information by an insider, as in

Edward Snowden's case, for example—and not "hacks," the penetration of an operating system or cyber-security system from a remote location.

If it had been a hack, they said, the NSA, due to its global surveillance capability, would have known long ago the precise location of the sender and receiver. It is unthinkable that the NSA would not be able to identify anyone—whether Russian or not—who tried to interfere in the U.S. election by hacking. Even the notorious John Bolton, himself a leading neocon, speaks of a "false flag" operation, and suspects that the American intelligence services hacked the Democratic Party's computers themselves, in order to be able to lay the event at Russia's doorstep.

In fact, a number of Trump's nominees for cabinet posts are people who know exactly where the bodies are buried when it comes to Obama's many activities

whitehouse.gov

President Barack Obama

that could one day become the subject of legal investigations. And so Obama's last stand is obviously also a gigantic maneuver to deflect from potential prosecution.

Otherwise, anyone who followed what was billed as Obama's last press conference saw someone who had absolutely nothing to say apart from unfounded allegations and "post-truth" assertions about the wonderful situation of the American economy. No vision. No perspective.

Germany Falls into Line

What then does it mean, in this campaign alleging Russian hacking, when Bruno Kahl, the new president of the German Federal Intelligence Service, the *Nachrichtendienst*, takes the same line as CIA Director John Brennan in declaring that there are "indications" of a trail leading to Moscow—thus obviously defending the neocons' line instead of the truth? What does it mean when the CDU/CSU demands a "hard line" against Moscow in connection with the alleged cyber-attacks?

It doesn't bode well. The notoriously pro-British Anne Applebaum, the *Washington Post* columnist, is "100% sure" that the Russian government will try to steal victory from Merkel in the 2017 German elections, "exactly as it did with its intervention against Hillary Clinton."

It has become clear since German Defense Minister von der Leyen expressed her "deep shock" over Trump's election, that many of the proponents of the failed paradigm of neoliberal globalization are not part of the geopolitical campaign against Russia and China because they get orders from Wall Street and the City of London, as many had assumed, but because geopolitics is a fundamental axiom of their identity.

The Syrian government had to resort to a military solution, with the support of Russia and Iran, to free Aleppo and other parts of Syria from ISIS, al-Nusra, and other terrorist groups, because Obama's continued arming of such groups ruled out any other possibility. Anyone who speaks of the "fall" of Aleppo, and not its liberation, is apparently siding with ISIS, the group re-

YouTube/DW

German Development Minister Gerd Müller at a South Sudan refugee camp.

sponsible not only for countless deaths in the Middle East, but also for the terrorist attacks in France and Germany.

Of course, the tragedy of war is that, in its course horrors occur—especially when it rages on for many years and is a proxy war instigated from the outside—horrors that produce a never-ending chain of horrors. It is therefore all the more urgent now that all neighbors of the Middle East—Russia, China, India, Iran, Egypt, but also Germany, France, and Italy—put large-scale reconstruction of the entire Middle East on the agenda. Donald Trump's designated National Security Advisor, Gen. Michael Flynn (ret.), has spoken in favor of a Marshall Plan for the Middle East, but it can only succeed if all the major powers cooperate and provide real prospects for the future for the people of this devastated region.

The concrete approach to be taken has long since been proposed by the Schiller Institute in its Phoenix Program for the Reconstruction of Aleppo and the Extension of the New Silk Road to Southwest Asia.

It is obviously just as urgent and necessary to implement a comprehensive industrialization and development program for Africa. A first baby step in the right direction was just taken by German Development Minister Gerd Müller, who seeks to motivate German businesses to invest more in Africa. That is progress, at least compared to the funding projects of the NGOs, whose Sunday sermons on democracy and human rights have brought next to nothing. China, India, and Japan are already active in Africa with significant investments in infrastructure and industrial zones, while Africans speak openly among themselves of how the Europeans will soon be irrelevant on the continent unless their indifference toward Africa changes very quickly.

What Germany Could Do

Chancellor Merkel announced in a video message that Germany will make African development a major theme of the G-20 Summit next July in Hamburg, which Germany will chair. Preparations for this summit, and then the summit itself, could become a turning point for the reconstruction of the Middle East and the industrialization of Africa, but only if the German government adheres to the high standard set by China at the last G-20 summit in Hangzhou, where President Xi Jinping pledged that China is committed to industrializing Africa.

If, however, Merkel intends to approach the development of Africa from the mindset of "the great transformation and decarbonization of the world economy," laid out by Joachim "John" Schellnhuber, CBE, and Dirk Messner—in a Dec. 13 Berlin press conference,

in anticipation of Germany assuming the 2017 presidency of the G-20—then Germany will be discredited, the Asian countries will expand their influence in Africa, and Europe will marginalize itself. The worldwide revolution underway is directed against exactly that thinly disguised neocolonial policy, of which Schellnhuber is exemplary. Nor will it do any good for Messner to dream up a "new, modern narrative" for this policy.

But Germany could meet the challenges of the year 2017 in a very different way, namely, by taking up China's offer for win-win cooperation in building the New Silk Road. More than 100 nations and institutions are already participating in this, the greatest infrastructure program in history. *The New Silk Road Becomes the World Land-Bridge*, published by *EIR* and the Schiller Institute, provides a comprehensive program that includes the key projects required for overcoming underdevelopment in Africa, such as, for example, the Transaqua project to replenish Lake Chad.

Germany could decide to cooperate in realizing these projects, and become a force for the good in creating a new paradigm of cooperation for the common aims of mankind.

HELGA ZEPP-LAROUCHE

The End of Globalization

This is an edited transcript of a video presentation by the founder of the Schiller Institutes, Helga Zepp-LaRouche, to the Sixth Annual International Conference on Fundamental and Applied Problems of Sustained Development in the "Nature-Society-Man" System at the Dubna International University of Nature, Society, and Man, in Dubna, Moscow Region, Russian Federation. The conference—"Designing the World's Future"—took place Dec. 19-20, 2016. This video message was prerecorded on Dec. 5, 2016.

Helga Zepp LaRouche: Dear participants in the Dubna Conference, dear Professor Bolshakov:

I feel very honored that you are allowing me to again address your conference, especially at this extremely dramatic and exciting moment in history. We are experiencing right now a world revolution. We are seeing the collapse of the paradigm of globalization, and it is maybe an irony of history that this paradigm only lasted about 25 years. It started to come into being with the disintegration of the Soviet Union in 1991, and it was characterized by the idea that there should be a unipolar world, and therefore that it would be legitimate to topple governments which would not submit to this unipolar world, by means of regime change, color revolution, or even wars based on lies, as we have seen so plentifully in the Middle East.

The economic side of this globalization went along with neo-liberal monetarism, which created the condition where the rich became so rich that they don't know what to do with what they have accumulated; the middle class dropped into poverty; and for an increasing mass of poor people, they became so poor that despite many jobs or no job at all, they could not make ends meet.

This has been the reason that there was a revolt. First in June in Great Britain with the Brexit; this continued with the election of Donald Trump in the United States; and we just saw the "no" to the referendum in Italy, which had essentially the same reason: complete mistrust of the population against an establishment which has been completely out of sync with the interests of the common good and the common people. This revolution, I dare to predict, will continue until the injustices associated with it—which have killed many people either in war or by economic means—are corrected.

Alternative System Is Ready

The good news is that an alternative is already in place. You know that we were extremely engaged, in the same 25-year period, with the idea of building a Eurasian Land-Bridge, which we already in 1991 called the New Silk Road; that we have promoted this idea of a New World Economic Order based on principles of physical economy, as they were proposed by Mr. LaRouche for almost 50 years—that they should become the basis for a New World Economic Order.

Now after some many difficulties, finally, in September 2013, President Xi Jinping, in an address in Kazakhstan, put the New Silk Road on the international agenda. And what you have seen in the meantime is an unbelievable speed of cooperation among nations in Asia, but also in other parts of the world, all based on the principle of "win-win" cooperation, whereby naturally China is exporting the very successful Chinese model of economy. After all, China was able to develop its own economy in a period of only 30 years, to reach the point that the industrialized world needed almost 200 years to achieve. China is exporting this economic model, but it is doing so on the basis of a win-win conception; that is, the idea that all participating countries have equal benefits and advantages. It is the same idea as the Peace of Westphalia, that foreign policy can only succeed if it is in the interest of the "Other."

I know that in the beginning, there was a certain amount of debate in Russia, about whether this would be against Russian interests. But in the meantime, I think a very successful process has developed. In the latest stage, at the Vladivostok Eastern Economic Forum in September, with the participation of [President Xi,] President Putin, Prime Minister Abe from Japan, and many others, and 2,500 delegates from many Asian countries, there was a big integration of the "One Belt, One Road" policy with the Eurasian Economic Union. That integration is moving forward very, very rapidly. It now already involves more than 100 nations and international institutions. It involves integration of infrastructure and high-technology cooperation, especially in the field of energy and nuclear energy; it involves space cooperation; and it has become a very attractive dynamic. After Vladivostok, this integration continued at the G-20 summit in Hangzhou; it followed with the ASEAN conference in Laos; then it went to Goa, to the BRICS annual conference, in India; and the latest example was the APEC conference in Peru, where many Latin American countries are now joining this development.

This is an economic model which is already reaching Europe, with the 16+1 countries of Central and Eastern Europe, which are now all cooperating with China on the development of infrastructure. But it is very clear that you cannot work with China from Central and Eastern Europe, without going through Russia, and without Russia being part of this, so that it becomes a real peace order. The EU has been extremely "standoffish," not taking up President Xi Jinping's offer of win-win cooperation; they have also, naturally, not taken up President Putin's many, many offers for cooperation in Eurasian integration from the Atlantic to the Pacific.

But now with the election of Donald Trump, there may be a change in the situation.

New Potentials

This is not yet decided, but it is a potential. One thing is very clear: If Hillary Clinton had been elected, we would in all likelihood have been on a very short road to World War III. Very hopefully, this is changing, because Trump already had phone conversations with President Putin and President Xi, and said that he wants to normalize the relationship between Russia and the United States. That obviously is not enough, but Trump had also promised that he would implement Glass-Steagall, the banking separation law of Franklin D. Roosevelt, and that he would invest, in his first 100

days in office, in a $1 trillion infrastructure program for the United States, to make the infrastructure in the United States the most modern in the world. To carry that out, he has a big job to do, given that the infrastructure in the United States is completely falling apart; but this is potentially the solution.

Because—after the Schiller Institute published the 370-page book, *The New Silk Road Becomes the World Land-Bridge*—we added one more chapter—namely that the United States must join the New Silk Road, because the United States needs a massive infrastructure program. Now President-Elect Trump may understand that, for good reason—because he is a businessman, and as President Putin just noted, he has been successful, and probably will find his new responsibilities on a higher level. And as Madame Fu Ying, chair of the Foreign Affairs Committee of the National People's Congress, said recently at a conference in New York, the proposal by Trump for a U.S. infrastructure program can be a bridge to the New Silk Road and the "One Belt, One Road" policies. If that program can be successfully put on the agenda, there is indeed hope.

LaRouche's 'Four Laws'

Mr. LaRouche—who would have liked to also send you greetings, but he unfortunately has a severe cold right now, but he greets you anyhow—he has been emphasizing that the only way the world can get out of this present crisis requires at an absolute minimum, the implementation of his four basic laws.

The First Law is to go back to the banking separation of Glass-Steagall of Franklin D. Roosevelt, doing exactly what Roosevelt did in 1933: separating the investment banks from the commercial banks—to isolate the derivatives and the bad debt, the unpayable debt, and just stop the casino economy. If the investment banks have to close, that's all the better, because we really don't need this casino aspect of the economy.

The Second Law goes back to the idea of the National Bank, which first was defined by Alexander Hamilton, the first Secretary of the Treasury of the United States, and which basically implies the Third Law—the idea that a sovereign government has the right to issue credit, provided it only goes into productive investment. I think this is a very important point in Russia right now, because of the various economic heritages coming from the Yeltsin period, and the question of where the power to generate credit is located. I think this idea, for Russia, is extremely important: that the sovereign government has the right to issue credit—and I don't mean money, I don't mean reserves, I don't mean paper money on the financial open markets—I mean something completely different. I'm saying that the sovereign government has the right to issue credit lines for investment in those areas of the economy in which you would also invest if the economy were in good shape. This was exactly what not only Alexander Hamilton did, but also what Lincoln did with the greenbacks, but especially what Franklin D. Roosevelt did, by creating the New Deal, where the Reconstruction Finance Corporation, after the Glass-Steagall Act was implemented, issued credits for huge, large-scale infrastructure projects such as the Tennessee Valley Authority project and others, and with that, took the United States out of the Depression and made it, by the end of the Second World War, the most prosperous nation in the world. And it was exactly the same kind of credit mechanism which was used in Germany in the postwar period by the *Kreditanstalt für Wiederaufbau*, to finance investment and the reconstruction of Germany. And this led to the Economic Miracle, which everybody admired, in only a few years time.

In 1931, there was a presentation by Dr. Wilhelm Lautenbach before the Reichsministerium in Germany, which essentially proposed what Roosevelt proposed two years later in the United States. What Dr. Lautenbach said, is that you have the coincidence of a world depression and a world currency crisis, and the usual market mechanisms do not function any more. The only way this can be addressed is by the state: The state has the right and the power to issue credit, and provided that credit goes into real production, based on physical principles, then it is not inflationary, and that is the only way you can get the economy going.

That would also function in Russia today; there is no question about it: It would work if people left the idea of "money," and instead went to the idea of physical economy only. The Fourth Law, which LaRouche insists is absolutely crucial, is that you have to have a crash program for the development of fusion power and international space cooperation, because the world economy lacks qualitative increases in productivity as a result of the paradigm of globalization. Investment in basic research and development in the last 25 years was neglected to the point that the world economy today is not in a position to take care of the existing world population. And you can only remedy that by a gigantic leap in productivity, which must be the result of higher levels of energy flux-density in the production process, and the absolutely necessary next step in this direction is fusion power.

Thermonuclear fusion solves several problems at the same time, and as you know, breakthroughs were made with the stellarator in Greifswald in Germany during the past year, but also in the Chinese EAST model. All it needs is appropriate funding to get such a crash program to lead to the success and potential commercial use of fusion power. Fusion power would give you energy and raw materials security for the entire world, and it would also solve the problem of getting mankind a new form of propulsion for space travel, and in that way shorten the time tremendously, which is absolutely necessary if you want to go into longer spaceflights such as to Mars.

The Chinese are very advanced; for example, they want to land on the far side of the Moon next year, and they have invited many, many countries to join them in the Chinese Space Station, which will be ready in the year 2022. They intend to mine helium-3 from the far side of the Moon as a fuel for a fusion economy on the Earth.

This is all very exciting, and I think that the idea that mankind is the only creative species, and, as Mr. LaRouche has said many, many times, we are the only known creative species in the universe so far (that does not mean that we may not eventually find other intelligent beings from other galaxies, since there are about 2 trillion galaxies, so that's a big question), but I think we are on the verge of a completely new paradigm. If we go now for the kinds of scientific breakthroughs which are on the level of Albert Einstein—the question of what is the role of man in the universe, and how can we think about ourselves, our creative mentation, as the most developed aspect of the universe—then we can change the identity of humanity so that we become truly adult, and that we work together. Geniuses of different nations and different cultures can easily work together, like astronauts, who understand the common aims of mankind which we must pursue, and not geopolitical aims.

I think we are on the verge of such a new paradigm. I think if we all act together now, to use this potential of hopefully changing the United States, getting new cooperation between the United States and Russia, moving to a completely new model of economy, what many people have called the common destiny or common future of the one mankind, I think we have a great future ahead of us.